DSCR Airbnb Mortgage Loans

How to Qualify for Airbnb Properties Using Rental Income Instead of Personal Income

By Joseph G. Correa

Licensed Mortgage Broker, Finibi Mortgage

Copyright & Legal Notice

Published by Live Stronger Faster

The information provided in this book is for educational and informational purposes only and should not be construed as financial, legal, or tax advice. Readers are encouraged to consult with licensed professionals before making any financial or real estate decisions. The author and publisher assume no responsibility for any losses or damages incurred as a result of the use or misuse of the information contained in this publication.

First Edition, 2026

Table of Contents

Foreword

This book exists to break down that barrier completely. It is designed to show you, step by step, how to qualify for Airbnb investment properties using the income generated by the property itself rather than relying on your personal income, tax returns, or employment history. In a world where self-employment is rising, where investors are building multiple income streams, and where traditional W-2 income is no longer the standard, DSCR loans provide a new pathway—one that aligns perfectly with how modern entrepreneurs actually earn and grow wealth. Instead of asking, "How much do you make?" lenders begin asking a far more powerful question: "How much does the property make?"

At its core, a DSCR Airbnb mortgage loan is built around a simple but transformative concept known as the Debt Service Coverage Ratio. This ratio measures the relationship between a property's income and its expenses, determining whether the property can sustain its own debt. Unlike conventional lending, which focuses heavily on personal financial documents, DSCR lending shifts the focus to asset performance. This means that if your Airbnb property generates enough income to cover its mortgage, taxes, insurance, and other obligations, you can qualify—even if your personal income does not fit within traditional underwriting guidelines. This single shift in perspective opens the door for investors who were previously locked out of real estate opportunities.

As you move through this book, you will begin to understand that DSCR lending is not just a loan product—it is a strategy. It is a way of thinking about real estate that prioritizes cash flow, scalability, and financial independence. Instead of being limited by your personal income, you can begin to build a portfolio based on performance. One property leads to another, and another, creating a compounding effect that allows you to scale faster than ever before. This is the exact reason why many of today's most successful short-term rental investors rely heavily on DSCR financing as the foundation of their growth.

One of the most important concepts you will master in this book is how DSCR is calculated specifically for Airbnb properties. Unlike long-term rentals, where income is relatively stable and predictable, short-term rentals introduce variability. Nightly rates fluctuate, occupancy changes seasonally, and performance depends on factors such as location, amenities, marketing, and guest experience. Because of this, lenders must rely on different methods to estimate income, including short-term rental data platforms, historical performance reports, and market-based projections. Understanding how these numbers are calculated—and how to position your property to meet or exceed lender requirements—will give you a significant competitive advantage.

Another powerful aspect of DSCR Airbnb loans is the ability to qualify without traditional income verification. For many investors, especially those who are self-employed, own multiple businesses, or use aggressive tax strategies, showing high taxable income can be a challenge. DSCR loans eliminate this obstacle by focusing on the asset instead of the borrower. This means you can continue to optimize your taxes while still qualifying for financing. It also means that your growth is no longer tied to how you present your personal finances, but rather to how well you select and operate your properties.

However, with this flexibility comes responsibility. DSCR lending is not about cutting corners—it is about understanding how to structure deals intelligently. Lenders still evaluate credit, reserves, property quality, and market conditions. They want to see that you are not only capable of acquiring a property but also managing it successfully. This is why education is critical. The investors who succeed in this space are those who take the time to understand the numbers, analyze deals carefully, and position themselves as low-risk borrowers even within a flexible lending environment. Throughout this book, you will also gain insight into how appraisals work for Airbnb properties. Traditional appraisals often rely on long-term rental comparables, which can undervalue short-term rental income potential. DSCR lenders, on the other hand, may use alternative valuation methods, including short-term rental income analysis, market data reports, and specialized appraisal techniques that account for nightly rates and occupancy trends. Learning how to navigate this process—and how to present your property in the strongest possible way—can make the difference between approval and denial.

What makes this book different is its focus on practical application. This is not theory. This is not outdated information based on traditional lending models. This is a real-world guide built around the current landscape of Airbnb investing and DSCR financing. You will learn how lenders think, what they look for, and how to position yourself to get approved consistently. More importantly, you will learn how to use DSCR loans not just to acquire one property, but to build a scalable system that generates long-term income and financial freedom.

As you continue reading, you will begin to see that DSCR

Airbnb mortgage loans are not just about qualifying—they are about unlocking a new level of opportunity. They allow you to move faster, scale smarter, and operate with greater flexibility. They align your financing strategy with your investment strategy, creating a seamless path from acquisition to cash flow to expansion. This alignment is what separates casual investors from those who build true real estate empires.

There is also a mindset shift that must occur when working with DSCR loans. You are no longer just a borrower—you are an operator. You are responsible for the performance of your asset. This means understanding your market, optimizing your listing, managing expenses, and continuously improving your property's profitability. The better your property performs, the easier it becomes to qualify for additional financing. In this way, your success compounds over time, creating a cycle of growth that becomes increasingly powerful with each deal you complete.

In many ways, DSCR Airbnb loans represent the future of real estate financing. They reflect a broader shift toward asset-based lending, where performance matters more than paperwork. They recognize the realities of modern income structures and provide a solution that is both flexible and scalable. For investors who are willing to learn and adapt, this creates an unprecedented opportunity to build wealth on their own terms.

By the end of this book, you will have a clear understanding of how DSCR Airbnb mortgage loans work, how to calculate and improve your DSCR, how to qualify without traditional income, and how to position your deals for approval. More importantly, you will have the confidence to take action. Because knowledge alone is not enough—the true power comes from applying what you learn and using it to create real results.

This is your entry point into a new way of investing, a new way of qualifying, and a new way of thinking about real estate. The tools are here. The strategy is here. The opportunity is here. Now it is up to you to take the next step and turn that opportunity into a portfolio that produces income, freedom, and long-term wealth through the power of DSCR Airbnb mortgage loans.

Chapter 1

Understanding DSCR Airbnb Mortgage Loans — The Foundation of Property-Based Financing

The foundation of modern Airbnb investing begins with a fundamental shift in how lenders evaluate borrowers, and that shift is best represented through DSCR Airbnb mortgage loans. For decades, traditional lending has focused almost entirely on the borrower—income, tax returns, employment history, and debt obligations. While this system worked for salaried employees with predictable income, it created barriers for entrepreneurs, investors, and self-employed individuals whose financial profiles did not fit neatly into standard underwriting boxes. As the short-term rental market expanded and platforms like Airbnb transformed the way properties generate income, lenders were forced to adapt. DSCR loans emerged as a direct response to this evolution, offering a more flexible and performance-based approach to financing.

At the center of DSCR lending is a simple but powerful idea: the property should be able to pay for itself. Instead of asking how much money you personally earn, lenders evaluate how much income the property produces relative to its expenses.

This creates a completely different pathway to qualification, one that aligns perfectly with the business model of Airbnb investing. When you operate a short-term rental, you are essentially running a hospitality business. Your property generates revenue through nightly bookings, and your success depends on your ability to manage occupancy, pricing, and guest experience. DSCR loans recognize this reality and treat the property as a standalone income-producing asset.

To fully understand DSCR Airbnb loans, it is important to grasp the concept of the Debt Service Coverage Ratio itself. This ratio measures the relationship between a property's gross or net income and its total debt obligations, including mortgage payments, taxes, insurance, and sometimes association dues. A DSCR of 1.0 means the property generates just enough income to cover its expenses. A DSCR above 1.0 indicates positive cash flow, while a DSCR below 1.0 suggests the property may not fully support its debt. Most lenders look for a DSCR of at least 1.0 to 1.25, depending on the program, property type, and borrower profile. The higher the ratio, the stronger the deal appears from a lender's perspective.

What makes Airbnb properties unique in this equation is the variability of income. Unlike long-term rentals, where a tenant pays a fixed monthly rent, short-term rentals operate on dynamic pricing. Nightly rates can change based on demand, seasonality, local events, and overall market conditions. This introduces both opportunity and complexity. On one hand, Airbnb properties often generate significantly higher income than long-term rentals, especially in high-demand markets. On the other hand, lenders must rely on projections and data analysis rather than fixed lease agreements. This is where specialized tools and appraisal methods come into play, allowing lenders to estimate income using historical performance, comparable short-term rental data, and market analytics.

Another defining characteristic of DSCR Airbnb loans is the reduced emphasis on personal income verification. In many cases, borrowers are not required to provide tax returns, W-2s, or pay stubs. This is particularly advantageous for self-employed individuals who may write off expenses to reduce taxable income, making it difficult to qualify under traditional guidelines. With DSCR loans, the focus shifts entirely to the asset. As long as the property meets the required DSCR threshold and the borrower meets basic credit and reserve requirements, approval becomes much more achievable. This opens the door for a wider range of investors, including those who are building businesses, scaling portfolios, or transitioning into full-time real estate investing. However, this flexibility does not mean that DSCR loans are easy or risk-free. Lenders still assess the overall risk of the transaction, including the borrower's credit score, liquidity, and experience. They also evaluate the property's location, condition, and market demand. A poorly chosen property in a weak market may struggle to generate sufficient income, regardless of the financing structure. This is why successful DSCR investors focus heavily on deal selection. They analyze potential revenue, occupancy rates, and operating expenses before making a purchase, ensuring that the numbers support both loan approval and long-term profitability.

One of the most important shifts you must make as an investor is to think like a lender. When you evaluate a deal, you should ask yourself the same questions a lender would ask. Does this property generate enough income to cover its expenses? Is there a margin of safety in case occupancy drops or expenses increase? How does this property compare to others in the same market? By adopting this mindset, you not only increase your chances of approval but also position yourself for sustainable success. DSCR lending rewards disciplined, data-driven investors who understand how to balance risk and reward.

Another key advantage of DSCR Airbnb loans is scalability. Because these loans are based on property performance rather than personal income, they allow investors to acquire multiple properties without being limited by debt-to-income ratios. In traditional lending, your ability to borrow decreases as you take on more debt. With DSCR loans, each property is evaluated independently, meaning one successful investment can lead to another, and another, creating a compounding effect. This is one of the primary reasons why DSCR financing has become the preferred strategy for investors looking to build large portfolios of short-term rental properties.

It is also important to understand the role of reserves in DSCR lending. Lenders typically require borrowers to have a certain amount of cash reserves, often expressed as a number of months of mortgage payments. These reserves act as a safety net, ensuring that the borrower can continue to make payments even if the property experiences temporary income fluctuations. For Airbnb investors, maintaining adequate reserves is not just a requirement—it is a best practice. The short-term rental market can be unpredictable, and having a financial cushion allows you to navigate periods of lower occupancy without stress.

As you continue through this book, you will see that DSCR Airbnb mortgage loans are not just a financing tool—they are a strategic advantage. They allow you to align your financing with your investment goals, focusing on cash flow, scalability, and long-term growth. They give you the freedom to operate as a true investor, building a portfolio based on performance rather than personal limitations. Most importantly, they provide a pathway to financial independence that is accessible, flexible, and scalable.

This chapter serves as your foundation. It introduces the key concepts, principles, and mindset shifts that will guide you throughout the rest of this book. By understanding how DSCR Airbnb loans work and how lenders evaluate deals, you are already ahead of the majority of investors who approach real estate without this knowledge. From here, we will go deeper into the mechanics of DSCR calculations, income projections, and deal structuring, giving you the tools you need to confidently acquire and scale Airbnb properties using this powerful financing strategy.

DSCR Airbnb Loan in Action

Imagine an investor named Daniel who is looking to purchase a short-term rental property in a high-demand vacation market. The purchase price of the property is $500,000, and Daniel plans to use a DSCR Airbnb loan with a 20% down payment. This means he will invest $100,000 of his own capital and finance the remaining $400,000. The interest rate on the loan is 7.5% with a 30-year term, resulting in a monthly principal and interest payment of approximately $2,797. In addition to this, the property has monthly taxes of $500 and insurance costs of $200, bringing the total monthly debt obligation to $3,497.

DSCR=Monthly Rental IncomeTotal Monthly Debt ServiceDSCR = \frac{\text{Monthly Rental Income}}{\text{Total Monthly Debt Service}}DSCR=Total Monthly Debt ServiceMonthly Rental Income

Now, instead of asking how much Daniel earns personally, the lender focuses on the property's income potential. Based on short-term rental data and comparable properties in the area, the projected average daily rate is $250, and the expected occupancy rate is 70%. This means the property is expected to be booked approximately 21 days per month. Multiplying 21 days by the $250 nightly rate results in a projected monthly gross income of $5,250.

From this gross income, Daniel must account for operating expenses such as cleaning, property management, utilities, maintenance, and platform fees. These expenses total approximately $1,250 per month, leaving a net operating income of $4,000. This is the number that will be used to calculate the DSCR.

Using the DSCR formula, we divide the net operating income of $4,000 by the total monthly debt obligation of $3,497. This results in a DSCR of approximately 1.14. This means the property generates 14% more income than is needed to cover its debt obligations. While this is above the minimum threshold of 1.0, some lenders may require a higher ratio, such as 1.2 or 1.25, depending on the risk profile. However, many DSCR programs will approve deals at 1.14, especially if the borrower has strong credit and reserves.

Now, let's explore how small changes can impact this scenario. If Daniel improves the property's performance by increasing the average daily rate to $275 through better marketing, design, and guest experience, his monthly gross income increases to $5,775. After expenses, his net operating income rises to approximately $4,500. Dividing this by the same debt obligation of $3,497 results in a DSCR of 1.29. This significantly strengthens the deal, making it more attractive to lenders and providing a greater margin of safety.

Alternatively, consider what happens if occupancy drops to 60% due to seasonality or increased competition. In this case, the property would be booked for only 18 days per month, generating $4,500 in gross income at the original $250 nightly rate. After expenses, the net operating income would be approximately $3,250. Dividing this by the debt obligation of $3,497 results in a DSCR of 0.93, which falls below the acceptable threshold. This highlights the importance of conservative underwriting and maintaining reserves to handle fluctuations in performance. This example demonstrates how DSCR Airbnb loans are directly tied to property performance. Every decision—from pricing strategy to property management—affects your ability to qualify and succeed. By understanding these dynamics and actively managing your property to maximize income, you can not only secure financing but also build a portfolio that generates consistent cash flow and long-term wealth.

Chapter 2

How DSCR is Calculated for Airbnb Properties — From Data to Approval

Understanding how DSCR is calculated for Airbnb properties is one of the most important skills you can develop as a short-term rental investor. While the concept of DSCR may appear simple at first glance, the way it is applied to Airbnb properties introduces layers of nuance that can either strengthen or weaken your ability to qualify for financing. Unlike traditional rental properties, where income is fixed and predictable, Airbnb properties operate in a dynamic environment influenced by pricing strategy, occupancy trends, seasonality, competition, and guest demand. Because of this, lenders rely on a combination of data sources, projections, and standardized underwriting methods to determine whether your property meets DSCR requirements.

At its core, DSCR is a ratio that compares the income generated by a property to the total cost of servicing its debt. However, the most important question is not the formula itself—it is how the income number is determined. For long-term rentals, this is straightforward. A signed lease agreement provides a clear monthly rental amount. But for Airbnb properties, there is no fixed lease. Instead, lenders must estimate income based on market data, historical performance, and comparable short-term rental properties. This estimation process is where the true art and science of DSCR Airbnb lending comes into play.

Lenders typically use one of three primary methods to determine Airbnb income. The first is short-term rental market data, often sourced from platforms such as AirDNA or similar analytics providers. These platforms aggregate data from thousands of Airbnb listings and provide insights into average daily rates, occupancy levels, and monthly revenue projections for specific markets. By analyzing comparable properties in the same area, lenders can estimate how much your property is likely to generate. This method is widely used because it provides an objective, data-driven approach that reduces uncertainty.

The second method is historical income, which applies if the property is already operating as a short-term rental. In this case, lenders may review actual booking data, including past revenue, occupancy rates, and performance trends. This can be a powerful advantage if the property has a strong track record, as it demonstrates proven income rather than projected estimates. However, lenders may still apply adjustments to account for market changes, ensuring that the income used for underwriting is sustainable and not overly optimistic. The third method involves appraisal-based income analysis. Some DSCR lenders use specialized appraisals that include short-term rental income projections. These appraisals go beyond traditional valuation methods by incorporating market rent data for both long-term and short-term rental scenarios. The appraiser evaluates comparable properties, analyzes local demand, and provides an estimated income figure that can be used for DSCR calculations. This hybrid approach helps bridge the gap between traditional real estate valuation and modern short-term rental performance.

Once the income is established, the next step is determining the property's expenses. This includes not only the mortgage payment but also taxes, insurance, and sometimes association dues. In many cases, lenders focus primarily on the total monthly debt service, which is often referred to as PITIA—principal, interest, taxes, insurance, and association fees. Operating expenses such as cleaning, maintenance, and management are sometimes excluded from the DSCR calculation, depending on the lender, but experienced investors always account for these costs when evaluating deals to ensure true profitability.

One of the key differences between novice and experienced investors is how they approach these numbers. A novice may rely solely on lender projections, while an experienced investor performs their own independent analysis. They look at multiple data sources, adjust for seasonality, and apply conservative assumptions to ensure that the deal remains viable under different conditions. This level of diligence not only improves your chances of approval but also protects you from unexpected financial challenges after closing.

Seasonality plays a critical role in Airbnb income, and understanding it is essential for accurate DSCR calculations. Many markets experience fluctuations in demand throughout the year, with peak seasons generating significantly higher revenue than off-peak periods. Lenders typically average income over a 12-month period to account for these variations, but as an investor, you must go deeper. You should analyze monthly trends, identify peak and low seasons, and ensure that your property can sustain its debt obligations even during slower periods. This is where having adequate reserves becomes crucial.

Another important factor is pricing strategy. The average daily rate is not fixed—it can be optimized based on demand, competition, and property features. Investors who actively manage their pricing using dynamic pricing tools can often achieve higher revenue than static projections suggest. This creates an opportunity to improve DSCR not just through property selection but through operational excellence. In other words, your ability to manage the property effectively can directly impact your financing outcomes.

It is also important to understand how lenders handle conservative adjustments. In some cases, lenders may apply a haircut to projected income, reducing it by a certain percentage to account for uncertainty. For example, if market data suggests a monthly income of $6,000, a lender might use only $5,400 for DSCR calculations. While this may seem restrictive, it is designed to ensure that the property remains viable under less-than-ideal conditions. As an investor, you should always be aware of these adjustments and factor them into your analysis.

As you continue to build your understanding of DSCR calculations, you will begin to see patterns. Properties in strong markets with high demand, unique features, and effective management tend to produce higher DSCR ratios. Conversely, properties in oversaturated or seasonal markets may struggle to meet lender requirements. This is why location, property type, and market analysis are just as important as the financing itself. A great loan cannot compensate for a weak deal, but a strong deal can unlock powerful financing opportunities.

Ultimately, mastering DSCR calculations is about more than just qualifying for a loan. It is about developing the ability to evaluate opportunities with precision and confidence. It is about understanding how income is generated, how expenses are managed, and how these factors interact to create sustainable cash flow. When you can look at a property and quickly determine its DSCR potential, you gain a significant advantage in a competitive market. You can move faster, make better decisions, and position yourself for long-term success.

This chapter is designed to give you that foundation. By understanding how DSCR is calculated for Airbnb properties, you are equipping yourself with one of the most valuable tools in real estate investing. As we move forward, you will learn how to apply these concepts in real-world scenarios, refine your analysis, and use DSCR as a strategic lever to build and scale your Airbnb portfolio.

DSCR Calculation with Airbnb Data and Scenario Analysis

To fully understand how DSCR calculations work in real-world Airbnb investing, let's walk through a detailed example that demonstrates how different variables impact your ability to qualify for a DSCR loan. Imagine an investor named Sofia who is purchasing a short-term rental property in a popular tourist destination. The purchase price is $600,000, and she plans to put 25% down, resulting in a loan amount of $450,000. The interest rate is 7.25% on a 30-year fixed loan, which results in a monthly principal and interest payment of approximately $3,071. Property taxes are $600 per month, insurance is $250, and HOA fees are $150, bringing the total monthly debt service to $4,071.

DSCR=Net Operating IncomeTotal Monthly Debt ServiceDSCR = \frac{\text{Net Operating Income}}{\text{Total Monthly Debt Service}}DSCR=Total Monthly Debt ServiceNet Operating Income

Now we turn to income. Based on short-term rental data, the average daily rate for comparable properties is $300, and the expected occupancy rate is 68%. This means the property is projected to be booked for approximately 20.4 days per month. Multiplying 20.4 days by the $300 nightly rate results in a gross monthly income of $6,120.

Next, we account for operating expenses. Sofia estimates monthly costs of $1,500, which includes cleaning, utilities, maintenance, supplies, and platform fees. This leaves a net operating income of $4,620. Dividing this by the total debt service of $4,071 results in a DSCR of approximately 1.13. This is slightly above the minimum threshold, making the deal potentially approvable depending on the lender's requirements.

Now let's analyze how different scenarios impact this DSCR. First, consider an improvement in pricing strategy. If Sofia enhances the property's design and marketing, increasing the average daily rate to $325 while maintaining the same occupancy, her gross monthly income rises to $6,630. After expenses, her net operating income increases to $5,130. Dividing this by the same debt service results in a DSCR of 1.26, significantly strengthening the deal.

Next, let's consider a drop in occupancy due to seasonality. If occupancy decreases to 55%, the property would be booked for approximately 16.5 days per month. At the original $300 nightly rate, this results in a gross monthly income of $4,950. After expenses, the net operating income drops to $3,450. Dividing this by the debt service of $4,071 results in a DSCR of 0.85, which would likely result in a loan denial. This highlights the importance of analyzing worst-case scenarios and maintaining reserves.

Now let's explore the impact of expense management. If Sofia reduces her operating expenses from $1,500 to $1,200 through better vendor negotiation and self-management, her net operating income increases to $4,920 at the original income level. This results in a DSCR of 1.21, which may meet stricter lender requirements. This demonstrates that DSCR is not only influenced by income but also by how efficiently you manage costs.

Finally, consider a lender applying a 10% income reduction for conservatism. Instead of using the projected $6,120 gross income, the lender uses $5,508. After expenses, the net operating income becomes $4,008. Dividing this by the debt service of $4,071 results in a DSCR of 0.98, which falls below the threshold. In this case, Sofia may need to increase her down payment, improve pricing, or choose a stronger market to qualify.

This example illustrates the dynamic nature of DSCR Airbnb lending. Every variable—pricing, occupancy, expenses, and lender adjustments—plays a critical role in determining your outcome. By understanding how these factors interact and actively managing them, you can position yourself for approval while building a property that generates consistent and reliable cash flow.

Chapter 3

No-Income Verification Strategy — How to Qualify Without Tax Returns Using DSCR Airbnb Loans

One of the most powerful advantages of DSCR Airbnb mortgage loans is the ability to qualify without traditional income verification. For decades, real estate financing has been built around a rigid framework that prioritizes tax returns, W-2s, and documented employment history. While this system works for salaried employees with stable income, it creates significant obstacles for entrepreneurs, self-employed individuals, and investors who structure their finances strategically. In today's world, where income can come from multiple sources—online businesses, investments, consulting, and digital products—the traditional model often fails to capture the true financial strength of a borrower. DSCR lending changes this completely by shifting the focus away from personal income and placing it on the performance of the asset.

At its core, the no-income verification strategy is about aligning your financing with your investment model. When you purchase an Airbnb property, you are not relying on a paycheck to make your mortgage payments. Instead, you are relying on the income generated by the property itself. DSCR loans recognize this reality and allow you to qualify based on the property's ability to produce cash flow. This creates a unique opportunity for investors who may not show high taxable income due to deductions, reinvestment strategies, or business structures. It also allows you to scale your portfolio without being limited by traditional debt-to-income ratios, which can quickly become restrictive as you acquire more properties.

To successfully implement a no-income verification strategy, you must understand what lenders are looking for in place of traditional income documentation. While DSCR loans eliminate the need for tax returns, they do not eliminate risk assessment. Lenders still evaluate your credit score, liquidity, reserves, and overall financial profile. A strong credit score demonstrates your ability to manage debt responsibly, while sufficient reserves show that you can handle temporary fluctuations in property income. These factors become even more important in the absence of income verification, as they provide lenders with confidence that you can sustain the investment.

Another key component of this strategy is property selection. Because the loan is based on the property's income, choosing the right property is critical. A high-performing Airbnb in a strong market can easily meet DSCR requirements, while a poorly chosen property may struggle to qualify regardless of your financial strength. This means you must approach each deal with a data-driven mindset, analyzing projected income, occupancy rates, and operating expenses. The goal is to ensure that the property not only meets lender requirements but also generates sufficient cash flow to support your long-term investment strategy.

Liquidity and reserves play a central role in DSCR lending, especially in no-income verification scenarios. Most lenders require a certain number of months of reserves, typically ranging from three to twelve months of mortgage payments. These reserves act as a safety net, ensuring that you can continue to make payments even if the property experiences a temporary decline in income. For Airbnb investors, this is particularly important due to the variability of short-term rental income. Seasonality, market conditions, and unexpected events can impact occupancy and revenue, making it essential to maintain a financial cushion.

Credit positioning is another critical factor. While DSCR loans are more flexible than traditional loans, they still require a minimum credit score, often in the range of 620 to 700 or higher depending on the program. A higher credit score can lead to better interest rates, lower down payment requirements, and more favorable loan terms. As an investor, you should view your credit profile as a strategic asset, actively managing it to maximize your borrowing power. This includes maintaining low credit utilization, making timely payments, and avoiding unnecessary debt.

One of the most misunderstood aspects of no-income verification DSCR loans is the role of documentation. While you are not required to provide tax returns or employment verification, you still need to provide detailed information about the property and the transaction. This includes the purchase contract, appraisal, insurance details, and sometimes a short-term rental income report. Lenders use this information to evaluate the viability of the deal and ensure that the property meets their underwriting criteria. Being organized and prepared can significantly streamline the approval process and increase your chances of success.

Another advantage of this strategy is the ability to separate your personal and investment finances. By qualifying based on the property rather than your personal income, you create a clear distinction between your personal financial life and your investment activities. This can provide greater flexibility and protection, allowing you to structure your investments in a way that aligns with your long-term goals. Many investors use business entities such as LLCs to hold their properties, further enhancing this separation and providing additional benefits such as liability protection and tax efficiency.

Scaling is where the no-income verification strategy truly shines. In traditional lending, your ability to acquire additional properties is limited by your debt-to-income ratio. As you take on more loans, your DTI increases, eventually reaching a point where you can no longer qualify for additional financing. DSCR loans eliminate this limitation by evaluating each property independently. This means you can continue to acquire new properties as long as each one meets the DSCR requirements. This creates a powerful pathway to portfolio growth, allowing you to build a collection of income-producing assets that generate consistent cash flow.

However, with this opportunity comes responsibility. The absence of income verification does not mean the absence of discipline. In fact, it requires even greater discipline, as you are relying entirely on the performance of your properties. This means you must be proactive in managing your listings, optimizing pricing, maintaining high occupancy, and controlling expenses. It also means being prepared for challenges, such as market fluctuations or unexpected repairs. The investors who succeed with this strategy are those who treat their properties as businesses, continuously improving performance and adapting to changing conditions. Risk management is another essential component. While DSCR loans provide flexibility, they also expose you to the realities of market performance. A property that performs well today may face increased competition or changing demand in the future. This is why diversification is important. By investing in different markets or property types, you can reduce your exposure to any single risk factor. Additionally, maintaining strong reserves and conservative underwriting assumptions can help you navigate uncertainties with confidence.

As you continue to develop your no-income verification strategy, you will begin to see that it is not just about qualifying for loans—it is about building a system. It is about creating a repeatable process for identifying opportunities, securing financing, and managing properties effectively. This system becomes the foundation of your real estate business, allowing you to scale with consistency and confidence. Each successful deal reinforces the system, making it easier to acquire the next property and the next.

Ultimately, the no-income verification DSCR strategy represents a shift in how real estate investing is approached. It moves away from reliance on personal income and toward a focus on asset performance. It empowers investors to take control of their financial future, building wealth through strategic acquisitions and effective management. By mastering this approach, you are not only unlocking access to financing—you are positioning yourself to create a scalable, sustainable, and highly profitable real estate portfolio.

Building a Portfolio Without Personal Income Using DSCR

To understand how the no-income verification strategy works in real life, consider an investor named Marcus who is self-employed and reports minimal taxable income due to business deductions. Under traditional lending guidelines, Marcus would struggle to qualify for a mortgage despite having strong cash flow from his businesses. However, by using DSCR Airbnb loans, he can qualify based on property performance rather than personal income.

Marcus identifies his first Airbnb property priced at $450,000. He puts 20% down, or $90,000, and finances the remaining $360,000 at a 7.5% interest rate over 30 years. His monthly principal and interest payment is approximately $2,517. Property taxes are $450 per month, and insurance is $200, bringing the total monthly debt service to $3,167.

DSCR=Property IncomeDebt ServiceDSCR = \frac{\text{Property Income}}{\text{Debt Service}}DSCR=Debt ServiceProperty Income

Based on short-term rental data, the property is expected to generate an average daily rate of $240 with a 72% occupancy rate. This results in approximately 21.6 booked days per month, producing a gross monthly income of $5,184. After accounting for operating expenses of $1,200, the net operating income is $3,984. Dividing this by the debt service of $3,167 results in a DSCR of 1.26, which meets most lender requirements.

With this approval, Marcus acquires the property and begins generating cash flow. Encouraged by his success, he looks for a second property. Because DSCR loans do not rely on his personal income, his first loan does not negatively impact his ability to qualify for another. He purchases a second property for $500,000 with similar terms. This property generates a DSCR of 1.30, further strengthening his portfolio.

Now, let's analyze the portfolio effect. Marcus now owns two properties, each generating positive cash flow. Combined, the properties produce a net operating income of approximately $8,000 per month, with total debt service of around $6,200. This results in a combined DSCR of approximately 1.29. While each property is evaluated independently for financing, Marcus benefits from the cumulative cash flow, which enhances his overall financial position.

Next, consider the role of reserves. Each property requires six months of reserves, calculated based on monthly debt service. For the first property, this is approximately $19,000, and for the second property, it is around $21,000. Marcus maintains these reserves in a separate account, ensuring that he can cover payments even during periods of lower occupancy. This not only satisfies lender requirements but also provides peace of mind.

Now let's explore a stress scenario. Suppose occupancy drops to 60% across both properties due to seasonal changes. The gross income for each property decreases, reducing net operating income. For the first property, NOI drops to $3,200, resulting in a DSCR of 1.01. For the second property, NOI drops to $3,500, resulting in a DSCR of 1.05. While still above 1.0, the margin is significantly reduced. However, because Marcus has reserves and diversified properties, he is able to navigate this period without financial strain.

Finally, consider the scaling potential. After successfully managing two properties, Marcus continues to acquire additional Airbnb investments using the same DSCR strategy. Each property is evaluated based on its own performance, allowing him to grow his portfolio without being limited by personal income. Over time, he builds a portfolio of five properties, each generating positive cash flow and contributing to his overall financial independence. This example illustrates the true power of no-income verification DSCR lending. It allows investors to bypass traditional limitations, focus on asset performance, and build scalable portfolios. By understanding the numbers, managing risk, and maintaining discipline, you can use this strategy to create a sustainable and highly profitable real estate business driven by the income of your properties rather than your personal earnings.

Chapter 4

Appraisal Methods for Airbnb Properties – Market Rent vs. Short-Term Rental Data

One of the most critical and often misunderstood components of DSCR Airbnb mortgage loans is the appraisal process. While many investors focus heavily on income projections, loan terms, and down payment strategies, the appraisal is the gatekeeper that ultimately determines how a lender views the value and income potential of a property. In traditional real estate transactions, appraisals are relatively straightforward. The appraiser compares the subject property to similar properties that have recently sold and, in some cases, analyzes long-term rental income. However, when it comes to Airbnb and short-term rental properties, this traditional approach does not fully capture the true earning potential of the asset. This is where specialized appraisal methods come into play, bridging the gap between conventional valuation and modern short-term rental performance.

At the heart of this chapter is the distinction between market rent appraisals and short-term rental income appraisals. Market rent refers to the estimated monthly income a property would generate if rented on a long-term lease. This is the standard approach used in conventional lending and is based on comparable rental properties in the area. While this method provides a stable and predictable income estimate, it often undervalues Airbnb properties, especially in high-demand markets where short-term rental income can significantly exceed long-term rent. For investors relying on DSCR loans, this can create a disconnect between the property's actual performance and the income used for underwriting.

Short-term rental data appraisals, on the other hand, are designed to capture the dynamic nature of Airbnb income. These appraisals incorporate data from platforms and analytics tools that track nightly rates, occupancy levels, and revenue trends for comparable short-term rental properties. Instead of relying solely on long-term lease comparables, the appraiser evaluates how similar properties perform as short-term rentals. This approach provides a more accurate representation of the property's income potential, which is essential for DSCR calculations. However, not all lenders or appraisers use this method, and understanding when and how it is applied is crucial for investors.

The choice between these two appraisal methods can have a significant impact on your ability to qualify for a DSCR loan. If a lender uses market rent and the resulting income is too low, the property may fail to meet DSCR requirements even if it performs exceptionally well as an Airbnb. Conversely, if short-term rental data is used, the higher projected income can improve the DSCR ratio and increase the likelihood of approval. This is why experienced investors pay close attention to lender guidelines and select financing partners who understand and support short-term rental investing.

Another important factor is the type of appraisal report used. Some DSCR lenders require a standard appraisal with a long-term rental analysis, while others offer specialized reports that include short-term rental income projections. These reports may include detailed breakdowns of average daily rates, occupancy trends, seasonal variations, and revenue estimates based on comparable properties. In some cases, the appraiser may use a combination of both methods, providing a range of income scenarios that can be used for underwriting. Understanding these options allows you to position your deal in the most favorable way.

Location plays a critical role in appraisal outcomes. Properties in well-established short-term rental markets with strong demand, tourism, and favorable regulations arc more likely to receive higher income projections. Appraisers in these markets have access to more data and comparable properties, making it easier to justify higher valuations. In contrast, properties in emerging or restricted markets may face challenges, as limited data and regulatory uncertainty can lead to more conservative estimates. As an investor, selecting the right market is just as important as selecting the right property.

Property characteristics also influence appraisal results. Features such as the number of bedrooms, unique amenities, design quality, and proximity to attractions can all impact a property's short-term rental performance. Appraisers consider these factors when selecting comparable properties and estimating income. For example, a well-designed property with a pool, modern furnishings, and strong branding may command higher nightly rates and occupancy compared to a basic property in the same area. By investing in upgrades and optimizing your property for guest experience, you can enhance both your income potential and your appraisal outcome.

Another key concept is the difference between projected income and stabilized income. Projected income is based on market data and assumptions, while stabilized income reflects the expected performance of a property after it has been fully optimized and operating consistently. Some lenders may use conservative projections, while others may consider stabilized income if there is sufficient evidence to support it. This distinction is important because it affects how your DSCR is calculated and whether your deal meets lender requirements.

It is also essential to understand how appraisers handle seasonality. In many Airbnb markets, income fluctuates throughout the year, with peak seasons generating significantly higher revenue than off-peak periods. Appraisers typically average income over a 12-month period to account for these variations, but the way this is done can vary. Some may use annualized data from comparable properties, while others may apply adjustments based on local trends. As an investor, you should analyze seasonal patterns in detail and ensure that your property can maintain sufficient income during slower periods.

Communication with your lender and appraisal team can make a significant difference in the outcome. Providing additional data, such as comparable Airbnb listings, revenue reports, and market analysis, can help support higher income projections. While appraisers must remain independent, presenting well-organized and relevant information can guide their analysis and ensure that your property is evaluated accurately. This proactive approach is often overlooked but can be a powerful tool in securing loan approval.

Another advanced strategy is selecting properties that perform well under both appraisal methods. While short-term rental data may provide higher income estimates, it is beneficial to choose properties that also have strong long-term rental potential. This creates a safety net, ensuring that the property remains viable even if market conditions change or regulations shift. It also provides flexibility, allowing you to pivot between short-term and long-term rental strategies if needed.

Risk management is a recurring theme in DSCR investing, and appraisals are no exception. Overestimating income can lead to approval challenges or financial strain after closing. Conservative underwriting, realistic projections, and thorough market analysis are essential for long-term success. By understanding how appraisals work and how different methods impact your DSCR, you can make informed decisions that balance opportunity and risk.

As you move forward in your Airbnb investing journey, mastering appraisal methods will become a critical skill. It is not enough to find a property with strong income potential—you must also ensure that this potential is recognized and validated through the appraisal process. This requires a combination of market knowledge, strategic planning, and effective communication. When done correctly, it allows you to unlock the full value of your property and maximize your financing opportunities.

This chapter provides the foundation for understanding how appraisals influence DSCR Airbnb loans. By learning the differences between market rent and short-term rental data, and by understanding how appraisers evaluate properties, you are better equipped to navigate the financing process with confidence. In the next sections, we will continue to build on this knowledge, exploring how to structure deals and optimize performance for long-term success.

Market Rent vs. Airbnb Appraisal Impact on DSCR

To see how appraisal methods directly affect your ability to qualify for a DSCR loan, let's walk through a detailed real-life example. Imagine an investor named Elena who is purchasing a property for $550,000 in a popular vacation market. She plans to put 20% down, resulting in a loan amount of $440,000. The interest rate is 7.25% on a 30-year loan, giving her a monthly principal and interest payment of approximately $3,000. Property taxes are $550 per month, insurance is $220, and there are no HOA fees, bringing her total monthly debt service to $3,770.

DSCR=IncomeDebt ServiceDSCR = \frac{\text{Income}}{\text{Debt Service}}DSCR=Debt ServiceIncome

Now let's compare two appraisal scenarios. In the first scenario, the lender uses a traditional market rent appraisal. Based on comparable long-term rental properties, the appraiser determines that the property would rent for $2,800 per month. Using this figure, the DSCR is calculated as $2,800 divided by $3,770, resulting in a DSCR of 0.74. This is well below the required threshold, and the loan would likely be denied under this method.

In the second scenario, the lender uses short-term rental data. Comparable Airbnb properties in the area show an average daily rate of $275 and an occupancy rate of 70%, resulting in approximately 21 booked days per month. This produces a gross monthly income of $5,775. After accounting for operating expenses of $1,300, the net operating income is $4,475. Dividing this by the same debt service of $3,770 results in a DSCR of 1.19. This meets most lender requirements and would likely result in loan approval.

Now let's analyze how small improvements can further strengthen the deal. If Elena enhances the property with better design and amenities, increasing the average daily rate to

$300, her gross monthly income rises to $6,300. After expenses, her net operating income increases to $5,000. This results in a DSCR of 1.33, providing a strong margin of safety and potentially better loan terms.

Next, consider a conservative lender adjustment. If the lender applies a 10% reduction to the projected income, the gross income used for underwriting becomes $5,670. After expenses, the net operating income is $4,370. Dividing this by the debt service results in a DSCR of 1.16, which is still acceptable but closer to the minimum threshold.

Now let's examine a seasonal downturn. If occupancy drops to 60%, the property is booked for 18 days per month at the original $275 nightly rate, resulting in a gross income of $4,950. After expenses, the net operating income is $3,650. Dividing this by the debt service results in a DSCR of 0.97, which falls below the threshold. This highlights the importance of reserves and conservative underwriting.

Finally, consider a hybrid strategy. If Elena selects a property that also performs well as a long-term rental, generating $3,500 per month instead of $2,800, the market rent DSCR improves to 0.93. While still below 1.0, it is closer to the threshold and provides additional flexibility. Combined with strong short-term rental performance, this creates a more resilient investment.

This example demonstrates how appraisal methods can dramatically impact your DSCR and loan eligibility. By understanding these differences and strategically selecting properties, lenders, and markets, you can position yourself for approval while maximizing income potential.

Chapter 5

Credit, Reserves, and Risk Positioning — How to Strengthen Your DSCR Airbnb Loan Approval

While DSCR Airbnb mortgage loans shift the focus away from personal income, they do not eliminate the need for strong borrower positioning. In fact, when income is removed from the equation, other factors become even more important. Credit, reserves, and overall risk profile move to the forefront of the underwriting process. These elements are what give lenders confidence that you can manage the loan successfully, even in the face of market fluctuations or temporary income disruptions. Understanding how to position yourself in these areas is critical not only for getting approved but also for securing better loan terms, lower interest rates, and higher leverage.

Credit is one of the most powerful tools you have as an investor. It serves as a direct reflection of your financial discipline and reliability. Even though DSCR loans do not require income verification, lenders still rely heavily on your credit score to assess risk. A higher credit score signals that you have a history of managing debt responsibly, making payments on time, and maintaining low levels of financial stress. This can translate into more favorable loan terms, including lower interest rates, reduced down payment requirements, and higher allowable loan amounts. Conversely, a lower credit score may result in stricter requirements, higher rates, or even denial in some cases.

It is important to understand that credit is not just about the score itself but also about the overall profile. Lenders look at factors such as payment history, credit utilization, length of credit history, and the mix of credit accounts. As an investor, you should actively manage these components to present the strongest possible profile. This includes paying all accounts on time, keeping credit card balances low relative to limits, avoiding unnecessary inquiries, and maintaining a healthy mix of revolving and installment credit. Over time, these practices can significantly improve your credit profile and enhance your borrowing power.

Reserves are another critical component of DSCR lending, particularly for Airbnb properties. Because short-term rental income can fluctuate, lenders want to ensure that you have sufficient funds to cover mortgage payments during periods of lower occupancy or unexpected expenses. Reserves are typically measured in months of mortgage payments, including principal, interest, taxes, and insurance. Depending on the lender and the risk profile of the deal, reserve requirements can range from three to twelve months or more. For example, if your monthly payment is $3,500 and the lender requires six months of reserves, you would need to show at least $21,000 in liquid or near-liquid assets.

Beyond meeting minimum requirements, maintaining strong reserves is a strategic advantage. It allows you to operate with confidence, knowing that you can weather temporary downturns without financial stress. It also positions you as a lower-risk borrower, which can lead to better loan terms. In many cases, lenders may be more flexible on DSCR thresholds or credit requirements if you demonstrate strong liquidity. This creates an opportunity to strengthen your overall profile by building and maintaining reserves over time.

Risk positioning is the combination of all the factors that influence how a lender perceives your deal. This includes your credit, reserves, property performance, market conditions, and overall investment strategy. The goal is to present a low-risk, high-confidence scenario that makes it easy for the lender to say yes. This requires a proactive approach, where you anticipate potential concerns and address them before they become obstacles. For example, if your DSCR is slightly below the ideal threshold, you might compensate by increasing your down payment, improving your reserves, or selecting a stronger market.

One of the most effective ways to improve your risk profile is through deal structuring. By adjusting key variables such as down payment, loan amount, and property selection, you can influence the overall strength of the deal. A larger down payment reduces the loan-to-value ratio, which lowers the lender's risk and improves your DSCR. Similarly, choosing a property with higher income potential or lower expenses can enhance your cash flow and make the deal more attractive. These adjustments may require more upfront capital or effort, but they can significantly increase your chances of approval and long-term success.

Another important aspect of risk positioning is market selection. Properties located in strong, high-demand markets with consistent tourism and favorable regulations are generally viewed as lower risk. These markets tend to have more stable occupancy rates and higher income potential, which supports stronger DSCR ratios. On the other hand, properties in uncertain or restricted markets may face additional scrutiny, as regulatory changes or limited demand can impact performance. As an investor, you should prioritize markets that align with lender preferences and demonstrate consistent short-term rental activity. Diversification is also a key strategy for managing risk. Instead of concentrating all your investments in a single market or property type, you can spread your portfolio across different locations and asset classes. This reduces your exposure to any single risk factor and creates a more balanced income stream. For example, you might invest in both urban and vacation markets, or in properties with different price points and target audiences. This approach not only enhances your financial stability but also makes you a more attractive borrower from a lender's perspective.

Another factor that lenders consider is your experience as an investor. While DSCR loans are accessible to beginners, having a track record of successful property management can strengthen your application. Experience demonstrates that you understand how to operate a short-term rental, manage guests, and maintain property performance. If you are new to Airbnb investing, you can still position yourself effectively by working with experienced property managers, building a strong support team, and presenting a well-thought-out business plan.

Insurance and property protection also play a role in risk positioning. Lenders want to ensure that the property is adequately protected against potential risks such as damage, liability, and loss of income. This includes having the appropriate insurance coverage and, in some cases, additional protections specific to short-term rentals. By addressing these factors proactively, you can further reduce perceived risk and strengthen your overall profile.

It is also important to consider the role of debt management. While DSCR loans allow you to scale without traditional income constraints, taking on too much debt too quickly can create financial strain. Responsible leverage is key. This means balancing growth with stability, ensuring that each property contributes positively to your overall portfolio. By maintaining a disciplined approach to debt, you can build a sustainable investment strategy that supports long-term success.

As you continue to develop your DSCR Airbnb investment strategy, you will begin to see how credit, reserves, and risk positioning work together to create a strong foundation. These elements are not separate—they are interconnected. A strong credit profile enhances your ability to secure favorable terms. Adequate reserves provide stability and confidence. Effective risk positioning ensures that your deals are structured for success. Together, they form the backbone of your financing strategy, enabling you to acquire properties, manage them effectively, and scale your portfolio over time.

This chapter emphasizes that while DSCR loans offer flexibility, they still require discipline and strategic planning.

By focusing on credit, reserves, and risk positioning, you can maximize your chances of approval and create a solid foundation for your Airbnb investment journey. As you move forward, these principles will guide your decisions, helping you navigate the complexities of real estate financing with confidence and clarity.

How Credit, Reserves, and Deal Structure Improve Approval

To understand how credit, reserves, and risk positioning impact DSCR loan approval, let's walk through a detailed example. Imagine an investor named Jason who is purchasing an Airbnb property for $520,000. He plans to put 20% down, resulting in a loan amount of $416,000. The interest rate is 7.5%, and the monthly principal and interest payment is approximately $2,910. Property taxes are $520 per month, and insurance is $220, bringing the total monthly debt service to $3,650.

DSCR=Net Operating IncomeDebt ServiceDSCR = \frac{\text{Net Operating Income}}{\text{Debt Service}}DSCR=Debt ServiceNet Operating Income

Based on short-term rental data, the property is expected to generate a gross monthly income of $5,800. Operating expenses are estimated at $1,300, resulting in a net operating income of $4,500. Dividing this by the debt service of $3,650 gives a DSCR of 1.23, which meets most lender requirements. Now let's examine how credit impacts this scenario. Jason has a credit score of 760, which qualifies him for better loan terms. Because of his strong credit, the lender offers a slightly lower interest rate of 7.25%, reducing his monthly payment to $2,800. This lowers his total debt service to $3,540. With the same net operating income of $4,500, his DSCR increases to 1.27. This improvement not only strengthens his approval chances but also increases his monthly cash flow.

Next, consider the impact of reserves. The lender requires six months of reserves, which for Jason equals $21,900. However, Jason has $50,000 in liquid assets. This strong reserve position reduces the lender's perceived risk and may allow for more flexibility in underwriting. For example, if his DSCR were slightly lower, the lender might still approve the loan due to his strong liquidity.

Now let's explore deal structuring. If Jason increases his down payment from 20% to 25%, his loan amount decreases to $390,000. This reduces his monthly principal and interest payment to approximately $2,730, lowering his total debt service to $3,500. With the same net operating income, his DSCR increases to 1.29. This demonstrates how a larger down payment can improve both DSCR and overall deal strength.

Next, consider a risk scenario where income decreases. If occupancy drops and net operating income falls to $4,000, Jason's DSCR with the original structure would be 1.10. While still above 1.0, it is closer to the minimum threshold. However, with the improved structure (lower interest rate and higher down payment), his DSCR would be approximately 1.14, providing a greater margin of safety.

Finally, let's look at the combined effect. By optimizing his credit, maintaining strong reserves, and structuring the deal strategically, Jason transforms a good deal into a strong one. His improved DSCR, lower monthly payment, and enhanced risk profile not only increase his chances of approval but also position him for long-term success.

This example highlights the importance of looking beyond the basic DSCR calculation. Credit, reserves, and deal structure are powerful levers that can significantly impact your outcome. By understanding and optimizing these factors, you can strengthen your applications, secure better terms, and build a resilient Airbnb investment portfolio.

Chapter 6

Scaling Your Airbnb Portfolio Using DSCR Loans — From One Property to Financial Freedom

Scaling is where DSCR Airbnb mortgage loans truly separate themselves from traditional financing. Many investors can acquire their first property, but very few understand how to systematically grow from one property into a portfolio that generates consistent, scalable income. The limitation is almost always financing. Traditional loans rely heavily on personal income and debt-to-income ratios, which quickly become restrictive as you take on more properties. DSCR loans eliminate this bottleneck by evaluating each property independently, allowing you to scale based on performance rather than personal financial limitations.

The first step in scaling is understanding that your initial property is not just an investment—it is a foundation. The goal is not simply to own one Airbnb property but to create a system that can be repeated. This means selecting a property that not only meets DSCR requirements but also produces strong, reliable cash flow. The income generated from this property can then be reinvested into future deals, creating a compounding effect that accelerates your growth. This is the essence of scaling: using one successful investment to unlock the next.

A key concept in scaling with DSCR loans is the idea of "deal independence." Each property stands on its own, meaning that its income and expenses determine its eligibility for financing. This is fundamentally different from traditional lending, where your personal income is the primary factor. With DSCR loans, your second, third, and fourth properties do not rely on your first property's debt. Instead, each property is evaluated based on its own DSCR ratio. This allows you to continue acquiring properties as long as each one meets the required criteria.

Cash flow management becomes increasingly important as you scale. While it may be tempting to focus solely on acquiring new properties, maintaining strong performance across your existing portfolio is essential. Each property must generate enough income to cover its expenses and contribute to your overall financial stability. This requires ongoing attention to pricing, occupancy, guest experience, and operational efficiency. As your portfolio grows, small improvements in performance can have a significant impact on your total income.

Another critical factor in scaling is capital allocation. Every deal requires an investment, typically in the form of a down payment, closing costs, and reserves. To scale effectively, you must manage your capital strategically, ensuring that you have enough liquidity to pursue new opportunities while maintaining adequate reserves for existing properties. This often involves reinvesting profits, leveraging equity, and optimizing your financing structure to maximize efficiency. The goal is to deploy your capital in a way that generates the highest possible return while maintaining financial stability.

Refinancing and equity extraction are powerful tools for scaling. As your properties appreciate in value and generate income, you can access this equity through cash-out refinances or other financing strategies. This allows you to recycle your capital, using it to fund additional acquisitions without relying solely on new savings. In the context of Airbnb investing, this strategy can be particularly effective, as high-performing properties often experience both income growth and value appreciation. By leveraging this equity, you can accelerate your portfolio growth and expand your investment reach.

Another important consideration is operational scalability. Managing one Airbnb property is relatively straightforward, but managing multiple properties requires systems and processes. This includes everything from booking management and guest communication to cleaning coordination and maintenance. As your portfolio grows, you may need to invest in property management services, automation tools, or a dedicated team to maintain efficiency. While this introduces additional costs, it also allows you to focus on higher-level strategy and growth.

Market selection plays a crucial role in scaling. Investing in multiple properties within the same market can provide efficiencies in management and operations, but it also increases your exposure to market-specific risks. Alternatively, diversifying across different markets can reduce risk but may require more complex management. The optimal strategy often involves a balance between concentration and diversification, allowing you to leverage local expertise while maintaining a resilient portfolio.

Financing strategy is another key component of scaling. While DSCR loans provide flexibility, each lender has its own guidelines, requirements, and limits. Some lenders may cap the number of loans per borrower, while others may have specific criteria for property types or locations. As you scale, it becomes important to build relationships with multiple lenders, ensuring that you have access to a variety of financing options. This not only increases your flexibility but also allows you to negotiate better terms and structure deals more effectively.

Risk management becomes increasingly important as your portfolio grows. While DSCR loans allow for rapid scaling, taking on too much risk can lead to financial instability. This includes overleveraging, underestimating expenses, or investing in volatile markets. To mitigate these risks, you should maintain conservative underwriting assumptions, build strong reserves, and continuously monitor your portfolio's performance. By balancing growth with stability, you can create a sustainable investment strategy that withstands market fluctuations.

Another powerful concept in scaling is the "portfolio effect." As you acquire more properties, your income streams become more diversified, reducing the impact of any single property's performance. For example, if one property experiences lower occupancy, the income from other properties can help offset the shortfall. This creates a more stable and predictable income stream, which is essential for long-term success. Additionally, lenders may view a well-performing portfolio more favorably, providing opportunities for better financing terms and increased leverage.

The mindset shift required for scaling is significant. You must transition from thinking like a single-property investor to thinking like a portfolio manager. This means focusing on systems, processes, and long-term strategy rather than individual transactions. It also means being proactive, continuously seeking new opportunities, and adapting to changing market conditions. The most successful investors are those who view scaling as a deliberate and strategic process, rather than a series of isolated deals.

Technology can also play a significant role in scaling. From dynamic pricing tools to property management software, there are numerous tools available to help you optimize performance and streamline operations. These tools can provide valuable insights into market trends, pricing strategies, and guest behavior, allowing you to make data-driven decisions. By leveraging technology, you can enhance efficiency, improve performance, and support the growth of your portfolio.

Ultimately, scaling your Airbnb portfolio using DSCR loans is about creating a system that works. It is about understanding the interplay between financing, operations, and market dynamics, and using this knowledge to build a portfolio that generates consistent income and long-term wealth. By focusing on performance, managing risk, and leveraging the flexibility of DSCR loans, you can move beyond the limitations of traditional financing and create a scalable, sustainable real estate business.

This chapter provides the blueprint for that process. It shows you how to move from one property to many, how to manage the complexities of scaling, and how to position yourself for long-term success. As you continue your journey, these principles will serve as the foundation for building a portfolio that not only grows but thrives.

Scaling from One Property to Five Using DSCR

To illustrate how scaling works in practice, let's follow an investor named Alex who begins with a single Airbnb property and gradually builds a portfolio using DSCR loans. Alex purchases his first property for $400,000 with a 20% down payment, investing $80,000. The loan amount is $320,000 at a 7.5% interest rate, resulting in a monthly principal and interest payment of $2,237. Including taxes and insurance, the total monthly debt service is $2,800.

DSCR=Net Operating IncomeDebt ServiceDSCR = \frac{\text{Net Operating Income}}{\text{Debt Service}}DSCR=Debt ServiceNet Operating Income

The property generates a gross monthly income of $5,000, with operating expenses of $1,200, resulting in a net operating income of $3,800. Dividing this by the debt service of $2,800 gives a DSCR of 1.36. This strong ratio allows Alex to secure the loan and begin generating cash flow.

After one year, Alex has accumulated $20,000 in additional savings from the property's cash flow. He uses this, along with additional capital, to purchase a second property for $450,000. This property generates a DSCR of 1.30, adding another stream of income to his portfolio. Now, Alex owns two properties with combined net operating income of approximately $7,800 and total debt service of $5,900, resulting in a combined DSCR of 1.32.

As Alex continues to scale, he purchases a third property for $500,000, followed by a fourth and fifth property over the next two years. Each property is evaluated independently using DSCR, allowing him to qualify without relying on personal income. By the time he owns five properties, his portfolio generates a total net operating income of $20,000 per month, with total debt service of $15,000. This results in a combined DSCR of approximately 1.33.

Now let's analyze the portfolio effect. If one property experiences a temporary decline in income, reducing its DSCR to 1.0, the overall portfolio DSCR remains above 1.25 due to the performance of the other properties. This demonstrates the stability created by diversification.

Next, consider the impact of refinancing. After several years, Alex's properties have appreciated in value, and he performs a cash-out refinance on one property, extracting $50,000 in equity. He uses this capital to fund the down payment for a sixth property, further accelerating his growth. Finally, let's examine a stress scenario. If market conditions reduce overall portfolio income by 15%, the net operating income decreases to $17,000 per month. With the same debt service of $15,000, the portfolio DSCR becomes 1.13. While lower, it remains above 1.0, allowing Alex to continue operating without financial distress.

This example demonstrates how DSCR loans enable scaling by focusing on property performance. By reinvesting cash flow, leveraging equity, and maintaining strong DSCR ratios, investors can build large, income-producing portfolios. The key is to approach scaling strategically, balancing growth with risk management and ensuring that each property contributes positively to the overall portfolio.

Chapter 7

Optimizing Airbnb Performance to Maximize DSCR — Pricing, Occupancy, and Profitability

As you progress deeper into the world of DSCR Airbnb investing, one principle becomes increasingly clear: your ability to qualify for financing and scale your portfolio is directly tied to how well your property performs. Unlike traditional real estate, where financing is often disconnected from operations, DSCR loans create a direct link between performance and opportunity. The better your Airbnb performs, the stronger your DSCR. The stronger your DSCR, the more financing options become available to you. This creates a powerful feedback loop where operational excellence fuels financial growth.

At the center of this process are three key drivers: pricing, occupancy, and expense control. These elements determine your revenue, your net operating income, and ultimately your DSCR. While many investors focus primarily on acquiring properties, the most successful investors understand that optimization is where the real value is created. A well-optimized property can significantly outperform market averages, turning an average deal into a high-performing asset that opens the door to additional financing and scaling opportunities.

Pricing strategy is one of the most impactful levers you can control. Unlike long-term rentals, where rent is typically fixed, Airbnb allows for dynamic pricing based on demand, seasonality, competition, and local events. This flexibility creates an opportunity to maximize revenue, but it also requires a strategic approach. Setting prices too high can reduce occupancy, while setting them too low can leave money on the table. The goal is to find the optimal balance where you maximize total revenue rather than focusing solely on nightly rates.

Dynamic pricing tools can play a significant role in this process. These tools analyze market data, competitor pricing, and demand trends to adjust your rates automatically. By using these tools, you can ensure that your property remains competitively priced while capturing higher rates during peak demand periods. This not only increases your average daily rate but also helps maintain consistent occupancy, both of which contribute to a stronger DSCR.

Occupancy is the second critical driver of performance. Even with high nightly rates, a property that sits empty for extended periods will struggle to generate sufficient income. Maintaining high occupancy requires a combination of effective marketing, strong listing optimization, and exceptional guest experience. This includes professional photography, compelling descriptions, responsive communication, and positive reviews. Each of these factors contributes to your property's visibility and attractiveness, increasing the likelihood of bookings.

Seasonality is an inherent aspect of Airbnb investing, and managing it effectively is essential for maintaining consistent occupancy. Different markets experience peak and off-peak seasons, and your strategy should adapt accordingly. During slower periods, you may need to adjust pricing, offer discounts, or target different types of guests to maintain bookings. Understanding these patterns and planning for them in advance can help you stabilize your income and protect your DSCR.

Expense management is the third pillar of optimization. While increasing revenue is important, controlling costs is equally critical. Operating expenses such as cleaning, maintenance, utilities, and platform fees can significantly impact your net operating income. By optimizing these expenses, you can improve your DSCR without necessarily increasing revenue. This might involve negotiating better rates with service providers, implementing energy-efficient solutions, or streamlining operations to reduce costs.

Another important aspect of optimization is property design and amenities. The way your property is presented can have a significant impact on both pricing and occupancy. Unique features, modern design, and thoughtful amenities can differentiate your property from competitors, allowing you to command higher rates and attract more bookings. This might include adding a hot tub, upgrading furnishings, or creating a distinctive theme that appeals to your target audience. These enhancements can lead to higher revenue and a stronger DSCR.

Guest experience is a critical factor that ties all these elements together. Positive reviews not only improve your property's ranking on Airbnb but also build trust with potential guests. This can lead to higher occupancy, better pricing power, and repeat bookings. Providing a seamless and enjoyable experience requires attention to detail, from the booking process to check-in, stay, and checkout. By consistently delivering high-quality experiences, you can create a competitive advantage that translates into financial performance.

Another advanced strategy is revenue diversification. In

addition to nightly bookings, you can explore additional income streams such as cleaning fees, pet fees, early check-in or late checkout options, and local experiences. While these may seem minor individually, they can add up over time and contribute to your overall income. This incremental revenue can improve your DSCR and enhance the profitability of your property.

Technology and automation play a significant role in optimization. From pricing tools to property management software, these tools can help you manage your operations more efficiently and make data-driven decisions. Automation can reduce the time and effort required to manage your property, allowing you to focus on strategy and growth. It can also improve consistency, ensuring that your property maintains a high standard of performance.

Benchmarking is another important practice. By comparing your property's performance to similar properties in your market, you can identify areas for improvement and set realistic goals. This includes analyzing metrics such as average daily rate, occupancy rate, revenue per available night, and guest ratings. By continuously monitoring these metrics, you can make informed adjustments and optimize your performance over time.

It is also important to consider the long-term impact of optimization. While short-term gains are valuable, the goal is to create a sustainable system that consistently produces strong results. This means balancing revenue growth with expense control, maintaining high standards of quality, and adapting to changing market conditions. By focusing on long-term performance, you can build a portfolio that remains resilient and profitable over time.

As you scale your portfolio, the principles of optimization become even more important. Small improvements in pricing, occupancy, or expenses can have a significant impact when applied across multiple properties. This creates a compounding effect, where incremental gains lead to substantial increases in total income. By applying these principles consistently, you can enhance the performance of your entire portfolio and strengthen your overall financial position.

Ultimately, optimizing Airbnb performance is about taking control of your investment. It is about understanding the factors that drive revenue and expenses, and using this knowledge to maximize your results. By focusing on pricing, occupancy, and profitability, you can improve your DSCR, secure better financing, and create a scalable, high-performing real estate portfolio.

How Optimization Increases DSCR and Unlocks Growth

To see how optimization directly impacts DSCR and investment performance, let's walk through a detailed example. Imagine an investor named Laura who owns an Airbnb property purchased for $480,000. She put 20% down, resulting in a loan amount of $384,000 at a 7.5% interest rate. Her monthly principal and interest payment is approximately $2,685. Including taxes and insurance, her total monthly debt service is $3,300.

DSCR=Net Operating IncomeDebt ServiceDSCR = \frac{\text{Net Operating Income}}{\text{Debt Service}}DSCR=Debt ServiceNet Operating Income

In the initial scenario, Laura sets her average daily rate at $220 with an occupancy rate of 65%. This results in approximately 19.5 booked days per month, generating a gross monthly income of $4,290. After operating expenses of $1,200, her net operating income is $3,090. Dividing this by her debt service of $3,300 results in a DSCR of 0.94, which is below the required threshold and would likely result in loan challenges.

Recognizing this, Laura decides to optimize her property. Shc upgrades the interior design, adds professional photography, and improves her listing description. She also implements a dynamic pricing tool to adjust her rates based on demand. As a result, her average daily rate increases to $250, and her occupancy rises to 72%. This results in approximately 21.6 booked days per month, generating a gross monthly income of $5,400.

After optimization, her operating expenses increase slightly to $1,300 due to higher occupancy and additional services. However, her net operating income rises to $4,100. Dividing this by her debt service of $3,300 results in a DSCR of 1.24, which meets most lender requirements and significantly improves her financial position.

Now let's analyze the impact of further optimization. Laura introduces additional revenue streams, such as pet fees and early check-in options, adding an extra $300 per month in income. Her gross monthly income increases to $5,700, and her net operating income rises to $4,400. This results in a DSCR of 1.33, providing a strong margin of safety and opening the door to additional financing opportunities.

Next, consider expense optimization. By negotiating better rates with her cleaning service and reducing utility costs, Laura lowers her monthly expenses to $1,150. This increases her net operating income to $4,550, resulting in a DSCR of

1.38. This demonstrates how both revenue and expense management contribute to improved performance.

Finally, let's examine a seasonal downturn. If occupancy drops to 60% while maintaining the optimized $250 nightly rate, Laura's gross monthly income decreases to $4,500. After expenses, her net operating income is $3,350. Dividing this by her debt service results in a DSCR of 1.02, which remains above the minimum threshold due to her optimization efforts. This example illustrates the power of optimization in DSCR Airbnb investing. By improving pricing, occupancy, and expense management, Laura transforms a weak deal into a strong, scalable investment. These improvements not only enhance her current property's performance but also position her to acquire additional properties and grow her portfolio.

Chapter 8

Refinancing and Cash-Out Strategies – Unlocking Equity to Scale Your Airbnb Portfolio

As your Airbnb portfolio begins to grow and your properties generate consistent income, one of the most powerful strategies available to you is refinancing. While many investors focus on acquisition, those who truly scale understand that equity is not meant to sit idle—it is meant to be leveraged. Refinancing and cash-out strategies allow you to unlock the value you have built within your properties and redeploy that capital into new opportunities. When combined with DSCR lending, this creates a powerful engine for growth, enabling you to scale faster without relying solely on new savings.

At its core, refinancing is the process of replacing your existing loan with a new one, typically with different terms. This can be done for several reasons, including lowering your interest rate, extending your loan term, or accessing equity through a cash-out refinance. In the context of Airbnb investing, the most important type of refinancing is the cash-out refinance, which allows you to convert a portion of your property's equity into liquid capital. This capital can then be used to fund additional property acquisitions, renovations, or other investments.

The concept of equity is central to this strategy. Equity is the difference between your property's current market value and the remaining balance on your loan. As your property appreciates in value and your loan balance decreases over time, your equity grows. In high-performing Airbnb markets, this growth can be accelerated by both market appreciation and increased income potential. Lenders recognize this value and allow you to access a portion of it through refinancing, typically up to a certain loan-to-value ratio, such as 70% to 80%.

One of the key advantages of using DSCR loans for refinancing is that the qualification process remains focused on property performance rather than personal income. This means that as long as your property generates sufficient income to meet DSCR requirements, you can refinance and access equity without the constraints of traditional income verification. This is particularly valuable for investors who are scaling their portfolios and may not have the personal income to support additional financing under conventional guidelines.

Timing is a critical factor in refinancing. The goal is to refinance when your property has both increased in value and stabilized in performance. Stabilization typically means that the property has a consistent track record of income, supported by booking history, occupancy rates, and revenue data. This provides lenders with confidence in the property's performance and supports higher valuations and income projections. Refinancing too early, before the property has reached this level of stability, may result in lower valuations and reduced access to equity.

Another important consideration is the impact of refinancing on your DSCR. When you increase your loan amount through a cash-out refinance, your monthly debt service will also increase. This means that your property must generate enough additional income to maintain an acceptable DSCR. As an investor, you must carefully analyze this trade-off, ensuring that the benefits of accessing equity outweigh the potential impact on your cash flow and risk profile. This requires a thorough understanding of your property's income potential and operating expenses.

The BRRRR strategy—Buy, Rehab, Rent, Refinance, Repeat—is particularly well-suited to Airbnb investing when combined with DSCR loans. In this approach, you acquire a property, improve it to increase its value and income potential, operate it as a short-term rental, and then refinance to extract equity. This process can be repeated multiple times, allowing you to build a portfolio using the same initial capital. The key to success with this strategy is executing each step effectively, from selecting the right property to optimizing its performance and timing the refinance appropriately.

Interest rates and market conditions also play a significant role in refinancing decisions. Lower interest rates can reduce your monthly payments and improve your DSCR, while higher rates may increase your debt service and reduce cash flow. As an investor, you should monitor market conditions and consider refinancing opportunities when they align with your financial goals. This may involve locking in lower rates, adjusting your loan terms, or strategically timing your cash-out refinance to maximize benefits.

Another powerful aspect of refinancing is the ability to consolidate or restructure your debt. For example, you may choose to refinance multiple properties into a single loan or adjust the terms of your existing loans to improve cash flow. While this approach requires careful planning and coordination, it can simplify your financial structure and enhance your overall portfolio performance. However, it is important to work with experienced lenders and advisors to ensure that these strategies are executed correctly.

Risk management remains a critical consideration when using refinancing strategies. While accessing equity can accelerate growth, it also increases your leverage and exposure to market fluctuations. Overleveraging can create financial strain, particularly if property income declines or expenses increase. To mitigate this risk, you should maintain conservative loan-to-value ratios, build strong reserves, and ensure that each property remains cash-flow positive after refinancing. This disciplined approach allows you to scale while maintaining financial stability.

Another important factor is the use of funds obtained through refinancing. The capital you extract should be deployed strategically, ideally into investments that generate higher returns than the cost of borrowing. This might include acquiring additional Airbnb properties, upgrading existing properties to increase income, or diversifying into other income-producing assets. By using your equity effectively, you can create a cycle of growth that continuously expands your portfolio and increases your overall income.

Tax considerations also play a role in refinancing strategies. While the specifics depend on your individual situation and local regulations, cash-out refinance proceeds are generally not considered taxable income because they are treated as loan proceeds rather than earnings. This can provide a tax-efficient way to access capital compared to selling a property and realizing gains. However, it is important to consult with a tax professional to understand the implications and ensure that your strategy aligns with your financial goals. As you continue to scale your Airbnb portfolio, refinancing becomes a key component of your overall strategy. It allows you to unlock the value you have created, reinvest it into new opportunities, and accelerate your growth. When used correctly, it transforms your properties from static assets into dynamic tools for wealth creation. By understanding the mechanics of refinancing, the impact on DSCR, and the importance of timing and risk management, you can leverage this strategy to build a scalable and sustainable real estate business.

This chapter provides the framework for using refinancing and cash-out strategies effectively. It highlights the importance of equity, timing, and disciplined execution, and shows how these elements come together to support long-term growth. As you move forward, these principles will help you make informed decisions, maximize your returns, and continue expanding your Airbnb portfolio with confidence.

Cash-Out Refinance to Acquire Additional Properties

To illustrate how refinancing and cash-out strategies work in practice, let's consider an investor named Daniel who owns an Airbnb property that has increased in both value and income.

Daniel originally purchased the property for $400,000 with a 20% down payment, resulting in a loan amount of $320,000. After two years of strong performance and market appreciation, the property is now valued at $520,000.

Daniel's current loan balance has been paid down to $310,000. This means he has $210,000 in equity ($520,000 minus $310,000). The lender allows a cash-out refinance up to 75% loan-to-value, which means Daniel can take out a new loan of $390,000 (75% of $520,000). After paying off the existing loan of $310,000, he is left with $80,000 in cash proceeds.

DSCR=Net Operating IncomeNew Debt ServiceDSCR = \frac{\text{Net Operating Income}}{\text{New Debt Service}}DSCR=New Debt ServiceNet Operating Income

Now, let's analyze the impact on his DSCR. Before refinancing, Daniel's monthly debt service was $2,800, and his net operating income was $4,200, resulting in a DSCR of 1.50. After refinancing, his new loan of $390,000 at a 7.5% interest rate results in a monthly payment of approximately $3,200. Including taxes and insurance, his total monthly debt service increases to $3,800.

With the same net operating income of $4,200, his new DSCR becomes 1.11. While lower than before, it still meets most lender requirements and allows him to access $80,000 in capital. Daniel uses this capital as a down payment for a second Airbnb property priced at $400,000. The second property generates a net operating income of $3,800 with a debt service of $2,900, resulting in a DSCR of 1.31. Now, Daniel owns two properties with combined net operating income of $8,000 and total debt service of $6,700, resulting in a portfolio DSCR of approximately 1.19.

Next, let's consider optimization. If Daniel improves the performance of his first property, increasing its net operating income to $4,500, his DSCR rises to 1.18. Combined with the second property, his portfolio DSCR increases to approximately 1.23, strengthening his overall financial position.

Now, let's analyze a stress scenario. If income from both properties decreases by 10%, the combined net operating income drops to $7,200. With the same debt service of $6,700, the portfolio DSCR becomes 1.07. While still above 1.0, the margin is reduced, highlighting the importance of reserves and conservative leverage.

Finally, consider the long-term impact. By using a cash-out refinance, Daniel was able to acquire a second property without saving additional capital. As both properties continue to generate income and appreciate in value, he can repeat this process, using equity to fund future acquisitions and scale his portfolio.

This example demonstrates how refinancing and cash-out strategies can accelerate growth in DSCR Airbnb investing. By carefully managing equity, analyzing DSCR impact, and maintaining a disciplined approach, investors can leverage their existing properties to build a larger, more profitable portfolio.

Chapter 9

Airbnb Mortgage Loans for Multi-Unit Properties — Scaling with Duplexes, Triplexes, and Fourplexes

As you advance in your Airbnb investing journey, one of the most powerful ways to accelerate both income and scalability is by transitioning into multi-unit properties. Duplexes, triplexes, and fourplexes offer a unique advantage that single-family properties cannot match: multiple income streams under one roof. When combined with DSCR Airbnb mortgage loans, these property types create an opportunity to significantly increase cash flow, improve risk diversification, and build a more resilient portfolio. However, they also introduce additional complexities that must be understood and managed effectively.

At the core of multi-unit Airbnb investing is the concept of income layering. Instead of relying on a single unit to generate revenue, you have multiple units contributing to the overall income of the property. This can dramatically increase your total revenue potential and improve your DSCR. For example, a duplex with two well-performing Airbnb units can often generate more combined income than a single-family property of similar value. This higher income can make it easier to meet lender requirements and create stronger cash flow.

One of the key advantages of multi-unit properties is their ability to balance risk. In a single-family Airbnb, if the property is vacant, your income drops to zero. In a multi-unit property, even if one unit is unoccupied, the other units can continue generating income. This creates a more stable and predictable revenue stream, which is particularly important in the context of DSCR lending. Lenders view properties with diversified income streams as less risky, which can improve your chances of approval and potentially lead to better loan terms.

However, qualifying for multi-unit Airbnb properties requires a deeper understanding of how income is evaluated. Lenders will typically assess the combined income from all units, using either market rent, short-term rental data, or a combination of both. The challenge is ensuring that each unit is optimized for performance and that the total income meets DSCR requirements. This means you must analyze each unit individually as well as collectively, considering factors such as occupancy, pricing, and operating expenses.

Another important consideration is zoning and compliance. Multi-unit properties are more likely to fall under stricter regulations, particularly when used for short-term rentals. Local laws may limit the number of units that can be rented on a short-term basis, require permits, or impose additional restrictions. As an investor, you must thoroughly research these regulations before purchasing a property, ensuring that your intended use aligns with local guidelines. Failure to do so can significantly impact your income potential and overall investment strategy.

Operational complexity is another factor that increases with multi-unit properties. Managing multiple units requires more coordination, from cleaning schedules and guest communication to maintenance and inventory management. While this can increase workload, it also creates opportunities for efficiency. For example, cleaning crews can service multiple units in one location, reducing costs and improving turnaround times. Similarly, centralized management systems can streamline operations and enhance overall performance.

Pricing strategy becomes even more important in a multi-unit context. Each unit may have different characteristics, such as size, layout, and amenities, which can influence pricing. You may choose to position units differently, targeting various guest segments to maximize occupancy and revenue. For example, one unit might cater to families, while another targets couples or business travelers. By diversifying your pricing strategy, you can capture a broader range of demand and optimize overall performance. Expense management also plays a critical role in multi-unit investing. While some costs may increase with additional units, others can be shared or reduced through economies of scale. For example, utilities, maintenance, and management costs may be more efficient when spread across multiple units. By carefully managing these expenses, you can improve your net operating income and strengthen your DSCR. This requires a detailed understanding of both fixed and variable costs and how they impact your overall financial performance.

Financing multi-unit properties with DSCR loans offers unique advantages. Because the loan is based on property income, the increased revenue from multiple units can support larger loan amounts and higher property values. This allows you to acquire more valuable assets without relying on personal income. However, lenders may also apply stricter requirements, such as higher DSCR thresholds or larger reserve requirements, due to the increased complexity of these properties. Understanding these requirements and preparing accordingly is essential for successful financing.

Another powerful strategy is combining short-term and long-term rental models within a multi-unit property. For example, you might operate some units as Airbnb rentals while leasing others on a long-term basis. This hybrid approach can provide a stable income base while allowing you to capitalize on the higher revenue potential of short-term rentals. It also offers flexibility, enabling you to adjust your strategy based on market conditions and regulatory changes.

Scaling with multi-unit properties can significantly accelerate your portfolio growth. Instead of acquiring multiple single-family properties, you can achieve similar or greater income with fewer transactions. This reduces acquisition costs, simplifies management, and allows you to build a larger portfolio more efficiently. Additionally, multi-unit properties often appreciate in value based on their income potential, creating opportunities for refinancing and equity extraction.

Risk management remains a critical consideration. While multi-unit properties offer diversification, they also require careful planning and execution. Overestimating income, underestimating expenses, or failing to comply with regulations can lead to financial challenges. To mitigate these risks, you should conduct thorough due diligence, use conservative projections, and maintain strong reserves. By approaching multi-unit investing with discipline and strategy, you can maximize its benefits while minimizing potential downsides.

As you transition into multi-unit Airbnb investing, your mindset must evolve. You are no longer managing a single property—you are operating a small hospitality business. This requires a higher level of organization, strategic thinking, and operational efficiency. However, it also offers greater rewards, including higher income, improved scalability, and increased financial stability. By mastering these concepts, you can unlock the full potential of multi-unit properties and take your Airbnb investing to the next level.

This chapter provides the foundation for understanding how multi-unit properties fit into your DSCR Airbnb strategy. By leveraging multiple income streams, optimizing performance, and managing complexity effectively, you can build a portfolio that is both scalable and resilient. As you continue your journey, these principles will guide your decisions and help you create a sustainable and profitable real estate business.

Duplex Airbnb vs Single-Family Property

To understand the power of multi-unit Airbnb investing, let's compare a single-family property with a duplex using DSCR calculations. Imagine an investor named Carla who is evaluating two properties, each priced at $500,000. She plans to put 20% down on either option, resulting in a loan amount of $400,000. The interest rate is 7.5%, and the total monthly debt service (including taxes and insurance) is $3,500.

DSCR=Total Net Operating IncomeDebt ServiceDSCR = \frac{\text{Total Net Operating Income}}{\text{Debt Service}}DSCR=Debt ServiceTotal Net Operating Income

First, let's analyze the single-family property. Based on market data, the property generates a gross monthly income of $5,200 as an Airbnb. Operating expenses are $1,300, resulting in a net operating income of $3,900. Dividing this by the debt service of $3,500 gives a DSCR of 1.11. While this meets minimum requirements, it provides a limited margin of safety.

Now, let's analyze the duplex. Each unit generates a gross monthly income of $3,200, resulting in a combined gross income of $6,400. Operating expenses are higher due to multiple units, totaling $1,800 per month. This leaves a net operating income of $4,600. Dividing this by the same debt service of $3,500 results in a DSCR of 1.31. This significantly stronger ratio improves loan eligibility and provides greater cash flow.

Next, consider a vacancy scenario. In the single-family property, if occupancy drops by 20%, the net operating income decreases to $3,200, resulting in a DSCR of 0.91. This falls below acceptable levels. In the duplex, if one unit experiences reduced occupancy while the other remains stable, the combined net operating income might decrease to $4,000, resulting in a DSCR of 1.14. This demonstrates the stability provided by multiple income streams. Now let's explore optimization. If Carla improves the performance of each unit in the duplex, increasing the average income to $3,400 per unit, the combined gross income rises to $6,800. After expenses, the net operating income becomes $5,000, resulting in a DSCR of 1.43. This strong ratio provides a significant margin of safety and opens the door to better financing terms.

Finally, consider scaling. By acquiring a duplex instead of a single-family property, Carla effectively doubles her income streams with one transaction. As she continues to invest in multi-unit properties, she can build a portfolio more efficiently, reducing acquisition costs and increasing overall income.

This example highlights the advantages of multi-unit Airbnb investing. By leveraging multiple units, investors can increase income, improve DSCR, and create more stable and scalable portfolios.

Chapter 10

Advanced Airbnb Mortgage Loan Structuring – Combining DSCR, Asset-Based, and Creative Financing

As you reach the advanced stage of Airbnb investing, the game shifts from simply qualifying for loans to strategically structuring deals. At this level, success is no longer determined by whether you can get approved—it is determined by how intelligently you combine financing tools to maximize leverage, cash flow, and long-term growth. DSCR loans remain the foundation, but when combined with asset-based lending and creative financing strategies, they unlock a new level of flexibility and opportunity. This is where investors transition from participants in the market to architects of their own financial ecosystem.

The essence of advanced structuring is flexibility. Instead of relying on a single loan product, you begin to layer different types of financing to achieve specific objectives. DSCR loans provide the core structure, allowing you to qualify based on property income. Asset-based loans allow you to leverage existing assets such as cash, stocks, or retirement accounts. Creative financing methods—such as seller financing, private lending, or partnerships—fill in the gaps, enabling you to close deals that might otherwise be out of reach. By combining these tools, you can tailor each deal to your unique situation and goals.

One of the most powerful combinations is DSCR financing paired with asset-based lending. For example, you might use a DSCR loan to finance the majority of a property's purchase price while using an asset-based line of credit to cover the down payment. This allows you to acquire properties without liquidating your assets, preserving your capital while still expanding your portfolio. The key is ensuring that the overall structure remains sustainable, with sufficient cash flow to cover all obligations.

Another advanced strategy is layering multiple properties within a broader portfolio structure. Instead of viewing each property as an isolated investment, you begin to manage your portfolio as a cohesive system. This includes optimizing the mix of loan types, balancing risk across properties, and strategically timing acquisitions and refinances. For example, you might use high-performing properties with strong DSCR ratios to offset or support newer acquisitions that are still stabilizing. This portfolio-level thinking allows you to scale more efficiently and manage risk more effectively. Creative financing plays a critical role in advanced structuring. Seller financing, for instance, allows you to negotiate terms directly with the property owner, potentially reducing your upfront capital requirements or securing more favorable terms. Private lenders can provide flexible funding for down payments or renovations, enabling you to move quickly in competitive markets. Partnerships can bring in additional capital or expertise, allowing you to pursue larger or more complex deals. Each of these strategies adds another layer of flexibility, expanding your ability to structure deals creatively.

Interest rate management is another important consideration. As you combine multiple financing sources, each with its own rate and terms, the overall cost of capital becomes a key factor. The goal is to balance leverage with affordability, ensuring that your cash flow remains strong while maximizing your return on investment. This may involve prioritizing lower-cost financing for core components of the deal while using higher-cost options strategically for short-term needs.

Loan-to-value (LTV) optimization is a central element of advanced structuring. By adjusting your down payment and leveraging additional financing sources, you can control your LTV and influence both your DSCR and overall risk profile. Higher leverage can accelerate growth but also increases risk, while lower leverage provides greater stability but requires more capital. Finding the right balance is essential, and it often varies depending on your goals, market conditions, and risk tolerance.

Another key concept is capital efficiency. Advanced investors focus not just on acquiring properties but on using their capital as efficiently as possible. This means minimizing idle funds, recycling equity through refinancing, and structuring deals in a way that maximizes returns relative to invested capital. By improving capital efficiency, you can achieve greater scale with the same amount of resources, accelerating your path to financial independence.

Timing and sequencing are also critical. The order in which you execute different components of a deal can impact both your financing options and overall outcome. For example, you might acquire a property using a bridge loan, stabilize and optimize its performance, and then refinance into a DSCR loan to secure long-term financing. This staged approach allows you to capture value at each step, turning underperforming assets into high-performing investments.

Risk management becomes even more important as your strategies become more complex. Each additional layer of financing introduces new variables, from interest rates and repayment terms to lender requirements and market conditions. To manage this complexity, you must maintain a clear understanding of your overall financial position, including cash flow, reserves, and exposure to risk. This includes stress-testing your deals, ensuring that they remain viable under different scenarios, and maintaining sufficient buffers to handle unexpected challenges.

Another advanced strategy is using business entities and structures to optimize financing. By holding properties in separate entities or using a portfolio-level entity, you can create additional flexibility in how you structure loans and manage risk. This can also provide benefits in terms of liability protection and tax efficiency, although it requires careful planning and coordination with legal and financial advisors.

Negotiation skills become increasingly important at this level. Whether you are working with lenders, sellers, or partners, your ability to negotiate terms can significantly impact your results. This includes negotiating interest rates, loan terms, purchase prices, and partnership agreements. Strong negotiation skills allow you to create win-win scenarios that align with your objectives while meeting the needs of other parties involved.

Technology and data analysis also play a role in advanced structuring. By leveraging data on market trends, property performance, and financing options, you can make more informed decisions and identify opportunities that others may overlook. This data-driven approach enhances your ability to structure deals effectively and stay ahead in a competitive market.

As you integrate these strategies, you will begin to see that advanced structuring is not about complexity for its own sake—it is about creating flexibility and control. It allows you to adapt to different situations, overcome obstacles, and capitalize on opportunities that might otherwise be inaccessible. It transforms your approach from reactive to proactive, enabling you to shape your investments rather than simply respond to them.

Ultimately, mastering advanced Airbnb mortgage loan structuring is about building a system that works for you. It is about combining the right tools in the right way to achieve your goals, whether that is rapid scaling, maximizing cash flow, or creating long-term stability. By understanding and applying these principles, you can elevate your investing strategy to a level where you are not just acquiring properties—you are building a sophisticated, scalable, and resilient real estate business.

Combining DSCR, Asset-Based, and Creative Financing

To illustrate how advanced structuring works in practice, let's consider an investor named Victor who is acquiring a high-performing Airbnb property priced at $700,000. Instead of using a single financing method, Victor combines multiple strategies to optimize his deal.

He secures a DSCR loan covering 75% of the purchase price, resulting in a loan amount of $525,000. At a 7.5% interest rate, his monthly principal and interest payment is approximately $3,670. Including taxes and insurance, his total monthly debt service is $4,400.

DSCR=Net Operating IncomeTotal Debt ObligationsDSCR = \frac{\text{Net Operating Income}}{\text{Total Debt Obligations}}DSCR=Total Debt ObligationsNet Operating Income

The property generates a gross monthly income of $8,000, with operating expenses of $2,000, resulting in a net operating income of $6,000. Dividing this by the debt service of $4,400 gives a DSCR of 1.36, which is strong and supports loan approval.

To cover the remaining 25% down payment ($175,000), Victor uses a combination of asset-based financing and private lending. He takes a $100,000 line of credit against his investment portfolio at a 6% interest rate, resulting in a monthly payment of approximately $500. He also secures a $75,000 private loan at 8% interest, with a monthly payment of $500. This brings his total additional monthly obligations to $1,000.

Now, we must recalculate his effective DSCR, considering all debt obligations. His total monthly obligations are now $5,400 ($4,400 DSCR loan + $1,000 additional financing). Dividing his net operating income of $6,000 by $5,400 results in an adjusted DSCR of 1.11. While lower than the initial DSCR, it remains above the minimum threshold and allows Victor to complete the deal with minimal out-of-pocket cash.

Next, consider optimization. If Victor improves the property's performance, increasing net operating income to $6,500, his adjusted DSCR rises to 1.20. This strengthens his position and provides a buffer against market fluctuations.

Now let's analyze a refinancing strategy. After two years, the property appreciates to $850,000, and Victor refinances at 75% LTV, resulting in a new loan of $637,500. He uses the proceeds to pay off the private loan and reduce his asset-based line of credit. His new monthly DSCR loan payment increases to $5,200, but his additional obligations decrease to $300. His total monthly obligations become $5,500.

With improved property performance generating $6,800 in net operating income, his new DSCR is approximately 1.24. This demonstrates how refinancing can simplify the structure and improve long-term sustainability.

Finally, consider a stress scenario. If net operating income drops to $5,800, his DSCR becomes 1.05. While still above 1.0, the margin is reduced, highlighting the importance of reserves and conservative structuring.

This example shows how combining DSCR, asset-based, and creative financing allows investors to acquire higher-value properties, optimize capital usage, and scale more efficiently. By understanding how each component impacts your overall DSCR and risk profile, you can structure deals that maximize both growth and stability.

Chapter 11

Risk Management and Long-Term Stability — Protecting Your Airbnb Portfolio While Scaling

As your Airbnb portfolio grows and your financing strategies become more advanced, one principle becomes increasingly important: protecting what you have built. While acquisition and scaling are exciting, long-term success in DSCR Airbnb investing depends on your ability to manage risk and maintain stability. Without a strong risk management framework, even a well-structured portfolio can become vulnerable to market fluctuations, operational challenges, and financial stress. This chapter is designed to help you think like a long-term investor, focusing not just on growth, but on sustainability, resilience, and control.

Risk in Airbnb investing comes from multiple sources, and understanding these risks is the first step toward managing them effectively. Market risk is one of the most significant factors. Changes in demand, competition, or local regulations can impact occupancy and pricing, directly affecting your income. For example, an increase in short-term rental supply in your market can lead to lower occupancy rates or reduced nightly rates. Similarly, regulatory changes can limit your ability to operate as an Airbnb, forcing you to adjust your strategy. Being aware of these risks and proactively monitoring your market is essential for maintaining stability.

Another major source of risk is income variability. Unlike long-term rentals, Airbnb properties do not provide consistent monthly income. Instead, revenue fluctuates based on seasonality, guest demand, and external factors such as economic conditions or travel trends. While this variability creates opportunities for higher income, it also introduces uncertainty. To manage this risk, you must adopt conservative underwriting practices, ensuring that your properties can sustain their debt obligations even during slower periods.

Financial risk is closely tied to leverage. While DSCR loans allow you to scale quickly, taking on too much debt can create pressure on your cash flow. High leverage increases your exposure to changes in income and expenses, making your portfolio more sensitive to market fluctuations. To mitigate this risk, you should maintain a balanced approach to leverage, avoiding overextension and ensuring that each property contributes positively to your overall financial position. This includes maintaining strong DSCR ratios, building reserves, and avoiding aggressive assumptions in your projections. Reserves are one of the most effective tools for managing risk. As discussed in earlier chapters, reserves provide a financial buffer that allows you to cover expenses during periods of lower income or unexpected costs. For Airbnb investors, this is particularly important due to the variability of short-term rental income. Maintaining reserves equal to several months of expenses for each property ensures that you can navigate challenges without disrupting your operations or financial stability.

Diversification is another key strategy for reducing risk. By spreading your investments across different markets, property types, and guest segments, you can reduce your exposure to any single risk factor. For example, if one market experiences a downturn, properties in other markets may continue to perform well, offsetting the impact. Similarly, diversifying property types—such as combining single-family homes with multi-unit properties—can create a more balanced and resilient portfolio.

Operational risk is often overlooked but plays a critical role in long-term success. This includes risks related to property management, guest experience, and maintenance. Poor management can lead to negative reviews, lower occupancy, and reduced income. To mitigate these risks, you must establish strong operational systems, whether through self-management or professional property management services. This includes maintaining high standards of cleanliness, responsiveness, and guest satisfaction, all of which contribute to consistent performance.

Insurance and liability protection are also essential components of risk management. Airbnb properties face unique risks, including property damage, liability claims, and loss of income due to unforeseen events. Ensuring that you have the appropriate insurance coverage, including short-term rental-specific policies, can protect you from financial losses and provide peace of mind. This is an area where cutting corners can lead to significant consequences, so it is important to invest in comprehensive coverage.

Another important aspect of risk management is stress testing your portfolio. This involves analyzing how your properties would perform under different scenarios, such as a decline in occupancy, an increase in expenses, or a rise in interest rates. By understanding how these factors impact your DSCR and cash flow, you can identify potential vulnerabilities and take proactive measures to address them. This might include adjusting your pricing strategy, reducing expenses, or increasing reserves.

Debt structure is another factor that influences risk. The terms of your loans, including interest rates, loan duration, and payment structure, can impact your financial stability. Fixed-rate loans provide predictability, while variable-rate loans may introduce uncertainty. As an investor, you should carefully consider the structure of your debt and how it aligns with your risk tolerance and long-term goals. In many cases, a balanced approach that combines stability with flexibility is ideal.

Another advanced concept is the importance of maintaining liquidity. While it may be tempting to reinvest all available capital into new acquisitions, maintaining access to liquid funds is essential for managing risk. This includes not only cash reserves but also access to credit lines or other sources of capital. Liquidity provides flexibility, allowing you to respond to opportunities or challenges without disrupting your overall strategy.

Market timing and adaptability are also critical. Real estate markets are cyclical, and conditions can change over time. Successful investors are those who can adapt to these changes, adjusting their strategies as needed. This might involve shifting focus to different markets, adjusting pricing strategies, or exploring alternative uses for your properties. By staying informed and flexible, you can navigate market changes and maintain long-term stability.

Another key element of risk management is discipline. It is easy to become overly aggressive during periods of strong performance, taking on more risk in pursuit of higher returns. However, this can lead to vulnerability when conditions change. Maintaining discipline means sticking to your underwriting criteria, avoiding overleveraging, and making decisions based on data rather than эмotions. This disciplined approach is what separates successful long-term investors from those who struggle to sustain their portfolios.

As your portfolio grows, the importance of systems and processes becomes more apparent. Managing multiple properties requires organization, efficiency, and consistency. This includes tracking financial performance, monitoring key metrics, and maintaining clear communication with your team. By implementing robust systems, you can reduce operational risk and ensure that your portfolio continues to perform at a high level.

Ultimately, risk management is about control. It is about understanding the factors that influence your success and taking proactive steps to manage them. By focusing on reserves, diversification, operational excellence, and disciplined decision-making, you can create a portfolio that not only grows but also withstands challenges. This is the foundation of long-term stability and financial independence.

Stress Testing and Risk Management in an Airbnb Portfolio

To understand how risk management works in practice, let's analyze a portfolio owned by an investor named Natalie. Natalie owns three Airbnb properties, each financed with DSCR loans. The combined monthly net operating income of her portfolio is $12,000, and her total monthly debt service is $9,000.

DSCR=Total Net Operating IncomeTotal Debt ServiceDSCR = \frac{\text{Total Net Operating Income}}{\text{Total Debt Service}}DSCR=Total Debt ServiceTotal Net Operating Income

In the baseline scenario, Natalie's DSCR is calculated as $12,000 divided by $9,000, resulting in a DSCR of 1.33. This indicates strong performance and provides a comfortable margin above the minimum requirement.

Now, let's stress test the portfolio. In the first scenario, occupancy decreases by 15% due to seasonal changes. This reduces her net operating income to $10,200. Dividing this by the same debt service of $9,000 results in a DSCR of 1.13. While still above 1.0, the margin is reduced, highlighting the importance of maintaining reserves.

In the second scenario, operating expenses increase by $1,000 per month due to higher maintenance and utility costs. This reduces her net operating income to $11,000, resulting in a DSCR of 1.22. This demonstrates how expense management impacts overall performance.

Next, consider a combined scenario where both income decreases and expenses increase. Net operating income drops to $9,500, resulting in a DSCR of 1.06. While still above 1.0, the portfolio is now much closer to the threshold, increasing financial risk.

Now let's examine the role of reserves. Natalie maintains $60,000 in reserves, equivalent to approximately six months of expenses. In a worst-case scenario where one property generates no income for two months, she can use her reserves to cover the shortfall without disrupting her operations.

Finally, consider diversification. If one property underperforms while the other two maintain strong performance, the overall portfolio DSCR may remain above 1.2. This demonstrates how multiple income streams can stabilize your financial position.

This example illustrates the importance of stress testing and proactive risk management. By understanding how different scenarios impact your DSCR and cash flow, you can prepare for challenges and maintain long-term stability in your Airbnb portfolio.

Chapter 12

Building a Complete Airbnb Investment System — From First Deal to Financial Freedom

At this stage of your journey, you have learned how to qualify for DSCR Airbnb loans, analyze deals, optimize performance, scale your portfolio, refinance for growth, and manage risk. Now it is time to bring everything together into a complete, repeatable system. This is the final and most important step—the transition from individual transactions to a structured, scalable business that generates consistent income and long-term wealth. The goal is no longer just to acquire properties, but to build a system that continuously identifies opportunities, executes deals, and maintains high performance across your entire portfolio.

A successful Airbnb investment system is built on five core components: deal sourcing, financing, execution, optimization, and scaling. Each of these components must work together seamlessly, creating a cycle that drives growth and stability. When this system is properly designed, it becomes self-reinforcing. One successful deal leads to another, and over time, your portfolio grows with increasing efficiency and confidence.

Deal sourcing is the starting point of the system. This involves identifying properties that meet your investment criteria and have the potential to generate strong DSCR. At this level, you are not randomly searching for properties—you are targeting specific markets, property types, and price ranges that align with your strategy. You analyze data, evaluate trends, and focus on opportunities that offer both income potential and long-term value. This disciplined approach ensures that every deal you pursue contributes to your overall system.

Financing is the engine that powers your system. DSCR loans provide the foundation, allowing you to qualify based on property income rather than personal income. As you progress, you incorporate additional strategies such as refinancing, asset-based lending, and creative financing to expand your options. The key is to maintain flexibility while ensuring that each deal is structured in a way that supports both growth and stability. This requires a deep understanding of how different financing tools interact and how they impact your DSCR and cash flow.

Execution is where your system comes to life. This includes everything from acquiring the property and completing any necessary renovations to setting up your Airbnb listing and launching operations. Efficiency is critical at this stage. The faster and more effectively you can execute, the sooner your property begins generating income. This requires organization, planning, and a clear process that can be repeated across multiple properties. Over time, you will refine this process, reducing costs, minimizing delays, and improving outcomes.

Optimization is the ongoing process of improving your property's performance. As discussed in previous chapters, this involves adjusting pricing, increasing occupancy, enhancing guest experience, and controlling expenses. Optimization is not a one-time effort—it is a continuous process that evolves with market conditions and guest preferences. By consistently improving your properties, you can increase your DSCR, enhance cash flow, and strengthen your overall portfolio.

Scaling is the final component that ties everything together. Once your system is in place, you can begin to replicate it across multiple properties. Each new acquisition follows the same process, benefiting from the experience and efficiencies you have developed. This creates a compounding effect, where your portfolio grows at an accelerating pace. Scaling is not about speed alone—it is about maintaining quality and consistency as you expand.

A critical aspect of building this system is documentation. Every step of your process should be clearly defined and documented, from deal analysis to property setup and management. This allows you to replicate your success and delegate tasks as your portfolio grows. Whether you are working with a team or managing everything yourself, having a documented system ensures consistency and reduces the risk of errors.

Another important element is team building. As your portfolio expands, you will need support to manage operations effectively. This may include property managers, cleaners, maintenance personnel, and administrative support. Building a reliable team allows you to focus on strategy and growth while ensuring that your properties continue to perform at a high level. The key is to establish clear roles, expectations, and communication processes that keep your operations running smoothly.

Technology plays a significant role in creating an efficient system. From property management software to dynamic pricing tools, technology can streamline operations, improve decision-making, and enhance performance. By integrating these tools into your system, you can automate repetitive tasks, track key metrics, and make data-driven decisions. This not only improves efficiency but also allows you to scale more effectively.

Another key component is performance tracking. To manage your portfolio effectively, you must monitor key metrics such as occupancy rate, average daily rate, revenue, expenses, and DSCR. By tracking these metrics, you can identify trends, detect issues, and make informed adjustments. This data-driven approach ensures that your system remains effective and continues to deliver strong results over time.

Capital management is also essential. As your portfolio grows, you must allocate your resources strategically, balancing reinvestment with reserves. This includes deciding how much to invest in new properties, how much to allocate for improvements, and how much to keep in reserve. Effective capital management ensures that you can continue to grow while maintaining financial stability.

Mindset is another critical factor. Building a successful Airbnb investment system requires discipline, patience, and a long-term perspective. There will be challenges along the way, from market fluctuations to operational issues. The key is to remain focused on your system, continuously improving and adapting as needed. By maintaining a strong mindset, you can navigate these challenges and stay on track toward your goals.

One of the most powerful aspects of a well-designed system is its ability to create freedom. As your portfolio grows and your processes become more efficient, your involvement in day-to-day operations can decrease. This allows you to focus on higher-level strategy, pursue new opportunities, or simply enjoy the benefits of the income you have created. This is the ultimate goal of Airbnb investing—not just financial success, but the freedom to live life on your own terms.

Another important consideration is legacy. A well-structured Airbnb portfolio can become a long-term asset that provides income for years to come. By building a strong system, you are not just creating income for yourself—you are creating a foundation that can be passed on or expanded in the future. This long-term perspective adds another layer of value to your investment strategy.

As you bring all these elements together, you will begin to see that success in Airbnb investing is not about individual deals—it is about the system behind those deals. It is about creating a process that consistently produces results, regardless of market conditions or individual circumstances. By focusing on building and refining your system, you can achieve a level of consistency and scalability that is not possible with a fragmented approach.

This chapter represents the culmination of everything you have learned. It provides the framework for turning knowledge into action and action into results. By implementing a complete Airbnb investment system, you can move beyond the limitations of traditional investing and create a scalable, sustainable, and highly profitable real estate business.

Building a System That Produces Consistent DSCR Growth

To illustrate how a complete Airbnb investment system works in practice, let's follow an investor named Sofia as she builds and scales her portfolio using a structured approach. Sofia starts with a single property purchased for $450,000 with a 20% down payment. Her loan amount is $360,000 at a 7.5% interest rate, resulting in a total monthly debt service of $3,200.

DSCR=Net Operating IncomeDebt ServiceDSCR = \frac{\text{Net Operating Income}}{\text{Debt Service}}DSCR=Debt ServiceNet Operating Income

In the initial phase, her property generates a net operating income of $4,000, resulting in a DSCR of 1.25. This meets lender requirements and provides a solid foundation. Through optimization, she increases her net operating income to $4,500, improving her DSCR to 1.41.

Using this success, Sofia applies her system to acquire a second property. This property generates a net operating income of $3,800 with a debt service of $3,000, resulting in a DSCR of 1.27. Now, her portfolio consists of two properties with a combined net operating income of $8,300 and total debt service of $6,200, resulting in a portfolio DSCR of 1.34. As Sofia continues to scale, she acquires a third and fourth property, each following the same process. Her portfolio now generates a total net operating income of $16,000 with total debt service of $12,000, resulting in a DSCR of 1.33. This consistency is a direct result of her system, which ensures that each property meets specific performance criteria.

Next, Sofia implements refinancing strategies to unlock equity and fund additional acquisitions. By extracting $60,000 from one property, she funds the down payment for a fifth property. This property generates a DSCR of 1.30, further strengthening her portfolio.

Now let's analyze a stress scenario. If her portfolio income decreases by 10%, her net operating income drops to $14,400. With the same debt service of $12,000, her DSCR becomes

1.20. While lower, it remains above the minimum threshold, demonstrating the resilience of her system.

Finally, consider long-term growth. By consistently applying her system, Sofia builds a portfolio of six properties, each generating strong DSCR ratios. Her total net operating income reaches $24,000 per month, with total debt service of $18,000, resulting in a DSCR of 1.33. This provides a stable and scalable income stream, allowing her to achieve financial independence.

This example demonstrates the power of a complete Airbnb investment system. By combining deal sourcing, financing, execution, optimization, and scaling into a repeatable process, investors can build portfolios that generate consistent income and long-term wealth.

Chapter 13

Exit Strategies and Long-Term Wealth — When and How to Cash Out, Hold, or Transition Your Airbnb Portfolio

As you build and scale your Airbnb portfolio using DSCR financing, it is easy to become focused entirely on acquisition, optimization, and growth. However, one of the most important aspects of long-term success is understanding how and when to exit—or more precisely, how to strategically transition your investments over time. Exit strategies are not about stopping; they are about evolving. They determine how you convert your portfolio into long-term wealth, liquidity, or lifestyle freedom. Without a clear exit strategy, even a highly successful portfolio can become inefficient or misaligned with your long-term goals.

At its core, an exit strategy is a plan for how you will realize the value of your investments. This can take many forms, including selling properties, refinancing to access equity, transitioning to long-term rentals, or holding assets for ongoing cash flow. The right strategy depends on your financial objectives, market conditions, and personal circumstances. For some investors, the goal is to build a portfolio that generates passive income indefinitely. For others, the goal is to accumulate assets and then liquidate them at the right time to achieve a significant financial milestone.

One of the most common exit strategies is the traditional sale. Selling a property allows you to realize its appreciation and convert your equity into cash. This can be particularly attractive in strong markets where property values have increased significantly. However, selling also comes with trade-offs. You lose the future income generated by the property, and you may incur taxes and transaction costs. As an investor, you must weigh these factors carefully, considering both the immediate benefits and the long-term implications.

Another powerful strategy is the hold-and-cash-flow approach. In this model, you retain ownership of your properties and continue to generate income over time. This approach aligns well with DSCR investing, as properties are selected and optimized for cash flow. By holding your properties, you benefit from both ongoing income and long-term appreciation. Over time, as loans are paid down and income increases, your cash flow can become substantial, providing financial stability and independence.

Refinancing, as discussed in earlier chapters, is another form of exit strategy—often referred to as a "partial exit." Instead of selling the property, you extract equity through a cash-out refinance, converting a portion of your investment into liquid capital while retaining ownership. This allows you to benefit from both immediate liquidity and continued income. It is a powerful tool for scaling and wealth building, but it must be used carefully to avoid overleveraging.

A hybrid strategy involves transitioning properties from short-term rentals to long-term rentals. This can be particularly useful in markets where regulations change or where short-term rental demand declines. By converting to long-term rentals, you can stabilize income and reduce operational complexity. While this may result in lower revenue compared to Airbnb, it also provides more predictable cash flow and reduced management requirements. This flexibility is one of the advantages of investing in properties that perform well under multiple rental models.

Another advanced exit strategy is portfolio consolidation. As your portfolio grows, you may choose to sell certain properties and reinvest the proceeds into fewer, higher-value assets. This can simplify management, reduce operational complexity, and increase overall efficiency. For example, you might sell several smaller properties and acquire a larger multi-unit property that generates similar or greater income. This approach allows you to optimize your portfolio while maintaining or increasing your cash flow.

Timing is a critical factor in any exit strategy. Real estate markets are cyclical, and the timing of your decisions can significantly impact your results. Selling during a peak market can maximize your returns, while holding during a downturn can allow you to benefit from future appreciation. Similarly, refinancing during favorable interest rate environments can improve your cash flow and access to capital. As an investor, you must stay informed about market conditions and be prepared to act when opportunities arise.

Tax considerations also play a significant role in exit strategies. Selling a property may trigger capital gains taxes, while refinancing typically does not. Additionally, strategies such as 1031 exchanges allow you to defer taxes by reinvesting proceeds into similar properties. Understanding these implications and working with a tax professional can help you structure your exits in a way that maximizes your net returns.

Another important consideration is lifestyle alignment. As your portfolio grows, your priorities may change. You may choose to reduce your workload, simplify your investments, or focus on other opportunities. Your exit strategy should reflect these changes, allowing you to transition your portfolio in a way that supports your desired lifestyle. This might involve selling certain properties, outsourcing management, or shifting to more passive investment models. Risk management is also a key component of exit planning. Holding properties indefinitely exposes you to market and operational risks, while selling too early may limit your long-term potential. The goal is to find a balance that aligns with your risk tolerance and financial objectives. This requires ongoing evaluation of your portfolio, including performance metrics, market conditions, and personal goals.

Another advanced concept is legacy planning. Real estate can be a powerful tool for building generational wealth, providing income and assets that can be passed on to future generations. By structuring your portfolio with this in mind, you can create a lasting financial foundation that extends beyond your own lifetime. This may involve estate planning, entity structuring, and long-term investment strategies designed to preserve and grow wealth over time.

As you consider your exit strategies, it is important to recognize that they are not mutually exclusive. You may use different strategies for different properties or at different stages of your journey. For example, you might sell some properties to realize gains, refinance others to access equity, and hold the rest for long-term income. This flexible approach allows you to adapt to changing circumstances and optimize your portfolio over time. Ultimately, exit strategies are about control. They allow you to determine how and when you realize the value of your investments, rather than being forced to react to external circumstances. By planning ahead and understanding your options, you can make decisions that align with your goals and maximize your results.

This chapter emphasizes that the end of one phase is the beginning of another. Whether you choose to sell, hold, refinance, or transition, your exit strategy is a critical part of your overall investment system. By approaching it with the same level of strategy and discipline as your acquisitions, you can ensure that your Airbnb portfolio continues to serve your financial and personal objectives for years to come.

Comparing Exit Strategies for an Airbnb Property

To understand how different exit strategies impact your financial outcomes, let's analyze a real-life scenario involving an investor named Daniel. Daniel owns an Airbnb property purchased for $400,000, which is now valued at $600,000 after several years of appreciation and optimization. His remaining loan balance is $300,000, and his monthly net operating income is $4,500. His total monthly debt service is $2,800.

DSCR=Net Operating IncomeDebt ServiceDSCR = \frac{\text{Net Operating Income}}{\text{Debt Service}}DSCR=Debt ServiceNet Operating Income

In the current scenario, Daniel's DSCR is $4,500 divided by $2,800, resulting in a DSCR of 1.61. This strong ratio reflects excellent performance and provides multiple options for his exit strategy.

First, let's consider selling the property. If Daniel sells at $600,000, he pays off his remaining loan of $300,000 and receives $300,000 in gross proceeds. After accounting for transaction costs and taxes, his net proceeds might be approximately $260,000. While this provides immediate liquidity, he loses the ongoing monthly cash flow of $1,700 ($4,500 NOI minus $2,800 debt service).

Next, consider a cash-out refinance. At 75% loan-to-value, Daniel can refinance the property at $450,000. After paying off the existing loan of $300,000, he receives $150,000 in cash. His new loan increases his monthly debt service to $3,600. With the same net operating income of $4,500, his DSCR becomes 1.25. This allows him to access capital while maintaining ownership and cash flow, albeit at a reduced level.

Now, let's analyze the hold strategy. If Daniel continues to hold the property, he maintains his current DSCR of 1.61 and monthly cash flow of $1,700. Over time, as the loan is paid down and income increases, his cash flow will grow, and his equity will continue to build. This provides long-term stability and wealth accumulation.

Next, consider a hybrid strategy. Daniel refinances to access $150,000 and uses this capital to acquire a second property. The new property generates a net operating income of $3,800 with a debt service of $3,000, resulting in a DSCR of 1.27. Combined, his portfolio now generates $8,300 in NOI with total debt service of $6,600, resulting in a DSCR of 1.26.

Finally, let's examine a stress scenario. If income decreases by 10% across both properties, total NOI drops to $7,470. With the same debt service of $6,600, the portfolio DSCR becomes 1.13. While lower, it remains above 1.0, demonstrating resilience.

This example highlights how different exit strategies impact both short-term and long-term outcomes. Selling provides immediate liquidity, refinancing offers a balance of liquidity and income, and holding maximizes long-term cash flow and appreciation. By understanding these options and their implications, you can choose the strategy that best aligns with your goals and financial vision.

Chapter 14

Building a Legacy with Airbnb Investing — Turning Cash Flow into Generational Wealth

At this point in your journey, you have moved beyond simply acquiring properties and generating income. You have learned how to qualify using DSCR loans, scale your portfolio, optimize performance, manage risk, and implement exit strategies. Now comes the final evolution: transforming your Airbnb portfolio into a legacy asset that extends far beyond your own lifetime. This is where short-term rental investing becomes more than a business—it becomes a vehicle for generational wealth, financial security, and long-term impact.

Legacy building begins with a shift in perspective. Instead of focusing solely on short-term profits or rapid scaling, you begin to think in terms of decades rather than years. You consider how your assets will perform over time, how they will be managed, and how they can be transferred or expanded in the future. This long-term mindset influences every decision, from property selection and financing to management and reinvestment strategies. It requires discipline, patience, and a clear vision of what you want to achieve. One of the most powerful aspects of Airbnb investing is its ability to generate both cash flow and appreciation. Cash flow provides immediate income, supporting your lifestyle and reinvestment efforts. Appreciation increases your equity over time, creating long-term wealth. When combined, these two elements create a compounding effect that can significantly increase your net worth. By reinvesting your cash flow into additional properties or improvements, you accelerate this process, building a portfolio that grows exponentially over time.

Debt plays a unique role in this process. While debt is often viewed as a liability, in real estate investing it can be a powerful tool for wealth creation. DSCR loans allow you to leverage your properties, using borrowed capital to acquire assets that generate income. Over time, as your tenants (or guests) effectively pay down your loans, your equity increases. This process, known as amortization, gradually shifts the balance from debt to ownership, strengthening your financial position. When managed responsibly, leverage allows you to build a larger portfolio than would be possible using only your own capital.

Another key component of legacy building is portfolio durability. This refers to your portfolio's ability to withstand market fluctuations and continue generating income over time. Durable portfolios are built on strong fundamentals, including high-quality properties, diversified markets, and conservative financial structures. They are designed to perform not just in ideal conditions, but also during periods of uncertainty. This resilience is essential for long-term success and ensures that your portfolio remains a reliable source of income for years to come.

Estate planning is an important aspect of legacy building. As your portfolio grows, you must consider how your assets will be managed and transferred in the future. This may involve creating trusts, structuring ownership through entities, or establishing clear guidelines for succession. The goal is to ensure that your assets are preserved and continue to generate value for future generations. While this requires careful planning and professional guidance, it is a critical step in transforming your investments into a lasting legacy.

Another important concept is income replacement. As your portfolio generates increasing cash flow, it can eventually replace your primary source of income. This creates financial independence, allowing you to choose how you spend your time and resources. For many investors, this is a key milestone—the point at which their investments provide enough income to cover their living expenses. Beyond this point, additional income can be reinvested, saved, or used to enhance your lifestyle. Scaling with intention is also critical.

While growth is important, it must be aligned with your long-term goals. This means focusing on quality over quantity, ensuring that each property contributes positively to your portfolio. It also means avoiding overleveraging and maintaining a balanced approach to risk. By scaling intentionally, you can build a portfolio that is both profitable and sustainable.

Another powerful strategy for legacy building is reinvestment. Instead of spending all your profits, you reinvest a portion into new opportunities or improvements. This creates a cycle of growth, where each property contributes to the acquisition of the next. Over time, this compounding effect can significantly increase your wealth. The key is to maintain discipline, consistently reinvesting and optimizing your portfolio.

Diversification continues to play an important role at this stage. By spreading your investments across different markets and property types, you reduce risk and create a more stable income stream. This is particularly important for legacy portfolios, as it ensures that your assets can withstand changes in market conditions. Diversification also provides flexibility, allowing you to adapt your strategy as needed.

Another important consideration is operational sustainability. As your portfolio grows, managing multiple properties can become increasingly complex. To build a lasting legacy, you must create systems and processes that ensure consistent performance. This may involve hiring property managers, implementing technology solutions, or building a team to support your operations. The goal is to create a system that can function effectively even without your direct involvement.

Tax efficiency is another key factor in maximizing your legacy. By structuring your investments strategically, you can minimize taxes and preserve more of your wealth. This may involve using strategies such as depreciation, refinancing, or tax-deferred exchanges. Working with experienced professionals can help you navigate these complexities and optimize your financial outcomes.

Another aspect of legacy building is impact. Beyond financial returns, your investments can have a broader impact on your community and the people around you. This might include providing high-quality accommodations, supporting local businesses, or creating opportunities for others. By aligning your investments with your values, you can create a legacy that extends beyond financial success.

As you approach this stage, your role as an investor evolves. You are no longer just acquiring and managing properties—you are building a system that creates long-term value. This requires a higher level of strategic thinking, focusing on how each decision contributes to your overall goals. It also requires a commitment to continuous learning and improvement, adapting to changes in the market and refining your approach over time.

Ultimately, building a legacy with Airbnb investing is about creating something that lasts. It is about using your knowledge, resources, and discipline to build a portfolio that provides financial security, independence, and opportunity for years to come. By focusing on long-term value, maintaining strong fundamentals, and aligning your strategy with your goals, you can transform your investments into a lasting legacy.

Turning an Airbnb Portfolio into Long-Term Wealth

To illustrate how an Airbnb portfolio can evolve into a legacy asset, let's examine the journey of an investor named Maria. Maria starts with a single property that generates strong cash flow and gradually builds a portfolio over time.

Maria's first property has a net operating income of $4,200 per month and a debt service of $3,000.

DSCR=Net Operating IncomeDebt ServiceDSCR = \frac{\text{Net Operating Income}}{\text{Debt

Service}}DSCR=Debt ServiceNet Operating Income Her DSCR is $4,200 divided by $3,000, resulting in a DSCR of 1.40. This strong ratio allows her to qualify for additional DSCR loans and begin scaling her portfolio.

Over the next five years, Maria acquires four additional properties, each generating similar performance. Her portfolio now consists of five properties with a combined net operating income of $21,000 per month and total debt service of $15,000. This results in a portfolio DSCR of 1.40.

Now let's analyze her cash flow. After covering debt service, Maria generates $6,000 per month in net cash flow. She reinvests a portion of this income into additional properties and improvements, further increasing her portfolio's value and income potential.

Next, consider the impact of loan amortization. Over time, Maria's loan balances decrease, increasing her equity. After 10 years, her total loan balance has been reduced by $200,000, while her property values have appreciated by $500,000. This results in a significant increase in her net worth.

Now let's examine a stress scenario. If her portfolio income decreases by 10%, her net operating income drops to $18,900. With the same debt service of $15,000, her DSCR becomes 1.26. While lower, it remains above the minimum threshold, demonstrating the resilience of her portfolio. Finally, consider long-term outcomes. As Maria continues to hold her properties, her loans are gradually paid off, and her cash flow increases. Once her properties are fully paid off, her monthly income increases to the full net operating income of $21,000. This provides financial independence and a stable source of income for the future.

This example demonstrates how Airbnb investing, when combined with DSCR financing and disciplined strategy, can create long-term wealth and financial security. By focusing on cash flow, appreciation, and reinvestment, investors can build portfolios that not only generate income but also serve as lasting legacy assets.

Chapter 15

The Final Blueprint — From Strategy to Execution and Lifelong Wealth Creation

As you reach the final chapter of this series, everything comes together into one unified principle: execution. Knowledge without execution creates no results. Strategy without action creates no income. The difference between those who build wealth through Airbnb investing and those who remain stuck in analysis is the ability to take what they have learned and apply it consistently, intelligently, and with discipline over time.

This chapter is not about new concepts—it is about integrating everything you have learned into a clear, actionable blueprint that you can follow for the rest of your investing career. From DSCR qualification and deal analysis to optimization, scaling, refinancing, and legacy building, you now have all the tools. What matters now is how you use them.

The first step in execution is clarity. You must define exactly what you are building. Are you aiming for $5,000 per month in cash flow? $20,000? Financial independence within five years? A legacy portfolio for your family? Your goal determines your strategy. Without a clear target, it is easy to drift, chase deals that do not align with your objectives, or scale in a way that creates stress rather than freedom. Clarity creates focus, and focus creates results.

Once your goal is defined, the next step is designing your acquisition plan. Based on your target income, you can determine how many properties you need and what level of performance each property must achieve. For example, if your goal is $10,000 per month in net cash flow and each property generates $2,000, you need five properties. This simple calculation becomes the foundation of your roadmap. From there, you can break down your plan into manageable steps, focusing on one acquisition at a time.

The next phase is deal discipline. Not every property is a good deal, and one of the biggest mistakes investors make is compromising their criteria in order to move faster. True execution is not about speed—it is about consistency. You must evaluate each deal based on DSCR, income potential, expenses, and market conditions, ensuring that it meets your standards. A single bad deal can set you back significantly, while a series of strong deals creates momentum that accelerates your growth.

Financing strategy remains central to execution. DSCR loans allow you to move forward without being constrained by personal income, but they still require careful planning. You must ensure that each deal meets lender requirements while maintaining strong cash flow. This includes managing your credit, reserves, and overall risk profile. As you scale, your financing strategy should evolve, incorporating refinancing, asset-based lending, and creative structures to maximize efficiency.

Execution also requires speed and efficiency. In competitive markets, opportunities do not last long. Being prepared—financially and operationally—allows you to act quickly when the right deal appears. This means having your financing lined up, your team in place, and your processes clearly defined. The faster you can move from analysis to acquisition to operation, the faster your property begins generating income.

Once a property is acquired, the focus shifts to optimization. This is where your deal truly becomes profitable. Pricing, occupancy, guest experience, and expense management all play a role in determining your net operating income. The goal is to maximize performance as quickly as possible, increasing your DSCR and strengthening your financial position. This not only improves your current cash flow but also positions you for future financing and scaling.

Consistency is the key to long-term success. One successful deal is valuable, but a repeatable system is transformational. By applying the same process to each property—sourcing, financing, execution, optimization—you create a cycle that drives continuous growth. Over time, this consistency leads to compounding results, where each property contributes to the acquisition of the next.

Scaling requires balance. While it is important to grow, it is equally important to maintain stability. This means managing risk, maintaining reserves, and avoiding overleveraging. Growth without stability can lead to financial stress, while stability without growth limits your potential. The goal is to find the balance that allows you to expand your portfolio while maintaining control and confidence.

Another critical aspect of execution is adaptability. Markets change, regulations evolve, and new opportunities emerge. Successful investors are those who can adapt to these changes, adjusting their strategies as needed. This might involve shifting to different markets, exploring new property types, or incorporating new technologies. By staying flexible and open to change, you can continue to grow regardless of external conditions.

Mindset plays a significant role in execution. Building a successful Airbnb portfolio requires persistence, resilience, and a willingness to learn from both successes and challenges. There will be obstacles along the way, from financing hurdles to operational issues. The key is to view these challenges as opportunities to improve and refine your system. A strong mindset allows you to stay focused and continue moving forward.

Another important element is time management. As your portfolio grows, your responsibilities increase. Managing multiple properties, analyzing deals, and coordinating operations can become demanding. To maintain efficiency, you must prioritize tasks, delegate where possible, and focus on high-impact activities. This allows you to scale without becoming overwhelmed.

The role of systems and automation becomes increasingly important at this stage. By implementing tools and processes that streamline your operations, you can reduce the time and effort required to manage your portfolio. This includes everything from automated messaging and pricing tools to financial tracking and reporting systems. These systems not only improve efficiency but also ensure consistency across your properties.

As you execute your plan, it is important to track your progress. This includes monitoring key metrics such as DSCR, cash flow, occupancy, and return on investment. By regularly reviewing these metrics, you can identify areas for improvement and make informed decisions. This data-driven approach ensures that your strategy remains aligned with your goals.

The final piece of the blueprint is longevity. The goal is not just to build a portfolio, but to sustain and grow it over time. This requires a long-term perspective, focusing on quality, stability, and continuous improvement. By maintaining strong fundamentals and adapting to changes, you can create a portfolio that generates income and wealth for years to come.

Ultimately, this chapter represents the transition from learning to doing. You now have the knowledge, the tools, and the strategies needed to succeed. What remains is execution. By taking consistent, disciplined action, you can turn your goals into reality and build a portfolio that provides financial freedom, stability, and long-term wealth.

Building a $20,000/Month Airbnb Income Portfolio

To bring everything together, let's walk through a comprehensive example of an investor named James who sets a goal of generating $20,000 per month in net operating income from Airbnb properties.

James determines that each property should generate approximately $4,000 in net operating income. Based on this, he plans to acquire five properties.

DSCR=Net Operating IncomeDebt ServiceDSCR = \frac{\text{Net Operating Income}}{\text{Debt Service}}DSCR=Debt ServiceNet Operating Income

For his first property, James purchases a home that generates $4,200 in net operating income with a debt service of $3,000, resulting in a DSCR of 1.40. This strong performance allows him to qualify for additional DSCR loans.

He repeats this process, acquiring four more properties with similar performance. His portfolio now generates a total net operating income of $21,000 per month with total debt service of $15,000. This results in a portfolio DSCR of 1.40.

Now let's analyze cash flow. After debt service, James generates $6,000 per month in net cash flow. This exceeds his initial goal and provides additional capital for reinvestment.

Next, consider optimization. By improving pricing and occupancy, James increases the net operating income of each property by $300 per month. This raises his total net operating income to $22,500, resulting in a portfolio DSCR of 1.50 and increasing his cash flow to $7,500 per month.

Now let's examine a stress scenario. If income decreases by 10%, his net operating income drops to $20,250. With the same debt service of $15,000, his DSCR becomes 1.35. This demonstrates the resilience of his portfolio.

Finally, consider long-term growth. As James continues to reinvest his cash flow and refinance his properties, he acquires additional properties, increasing his portfolio to eight properties. His total net operating income reaches $32,000 per month with debt service of $24,000, resulting in a DSCR of 1.33.

This example illustrates how a clear goal, combined with disciplined execution and DSCR financing, can lead to significant income and long-term wealth. By following a structured blueprint, investors can build scalable portfolios that generate consistent cash flow and financial independence.

Final Thoughts

The Journey from Knowledge to Financial Freedom

As you reach the end of this series, it is important to recognize that what you have gained is far more than information—you now possess a complete framework for building, scaling, and sustaining a profitable Airbnb investment portfolio using DSCR mortgage strategies. From understanding how lenders evaluate deals, to mastering income calculations, optimizing performance, managing risk, and structuring advanced financing, you have been equipped with the tools that many investors spend years trying to figure out. The difference now lies in what you choose to do with this knowledge.

At its core, this entire journey is about transformation. It is about shifting from a traditional mindset—where income determines opportunity—to a modern, asset-based mindset where performance determines growth. DSCR loans represent more than just a financing product; they represent a new way of thinking about real estate. They remove many of the barriers that have historically limited investors and replace them with a system that rewards strategy, discipline, and execution. This shift opens the door to opportunities that were once inaccessible, allowing you to build wealth on your own terms. One of the most important lessons throughout this series is that real estate success is not about a single deal—it is about a system. Anyone can get lucky with one property, but sustainable success comes from repeatable processes. The investors who build long-term wealth are those who create systems that consistently produce results. They know how to find deals, how to finance them, how to operate them, and how to scale them. More importantly, they refine these systems over time, improving efficiency and performance with each new acquisition.

Another key takeaway is the importance of discipline. In a world filled with opportunities, it is easy to become distracted or to chase deals that do not align with your strategy. Discipline means sticking to your criteria, analyzing deals carefully, and making decisions based on data rather than emotions. It means understanding that not every opportunity is the right opportunity, and that sometimes the best decision is to wait for the right deal. This level of discipline is what separates successful investors from those who struggle to achieve consistent results.

Risk management is equally important. While DSCR loans provide flexibility and scalability, they also require responsibility. The ability to qualify without traditional income does not eliminate risk—it simply shifts the focus to the performance of your properties. This means that your success depends on your ability to select strong deals, manage your properties effectively, and maintain financial stability. By building reserves, diversifying your portfolio, and using conservative assumptions, you can protect yourself from unexpected challenges and create a resilient investment strategy.

Optimization is where the true power of Airbnb investing is realized. Unlike many other forms of real estate, short-term rentals allow you to actively influence your income through pricing, marketing, and guest experience. This creates an opportunity to continuously improve your performance, increasing both your cash flow and your DSCR. Over time, these improvements compound, transforming average properties into high-performing assets that drive your portfolio forward.

Scaling is the natural progression of this process. Once you have established a strong foundation and a repeatable system, you can begin to expand your portfolio. DSCR loans make this possible by evaluating each property independently, allowing you to grow without being constrained by personal income. However, scaling must be approached with balance. Growth should be accompanied by stability, ensuring that your portfolio remains strong and sustainable as it expands. Another important aspect of this journey is adaptability. The real estate market is constantly evolving, influenced by economic conditions, technological advancements, and changing consumer behavior. Successful investors are those who remain flexible, adjusting their strategies to align with these changes. Whether it is adopting new pricing tools, exploring different markets, or adjusting to regulatory shifts, adaptability ensures that you remain competitive and continue to grow.

Mindset plays a critical role in your success. Building a profitable Airbnb portfolio is not a quick or easy process—it requires persistence, patience, and a willingness to learn. There will be challenges along the way, from financing hurdles to operational issues. The key is to view these challenges as opportunities for growth, using them to refine your system and improve your approach. A strong mindset allows you to stay focused and continue moving forward, even when faced with obstacles.

Another powerful concept is the idea of compounding. Each property you acquire contributes to your overall income and equity, creating a snowball effect that accelerates your growth. As your portfolio expands, your cash flow increases, providing additional capital for reinvestment. At the same time, your properties appreciate in value, further increasing your net worth. This compounding effect is what allows investors to achieve significant financial growth over time. Financial freedom is the ultimate goal for many investors, but it is important to understand what that means for you personally. For some, it may mean replacing their primary income and having the flexibility to choose how they spend their time. For others, it may mean building a legacy that provides for future generations. Whatever your goal, your investment strategy should be aligned with your vision, ensuring that your efforts lead to the outcomes you desire.

Another important consideration is the role of time. Real estate investing is not about instant results—it is about long-term growth. While you may see early success, the true power of your portfolio will be realized over years and decades. This requires patience and a commitment to the process, understanding that each step you take contributes to your long-term success.

As you move forward, it is essential to take action. Knowledge alone does not create results—execution does. The sooner you begin applying what you have learned, the sooner you will start building momentum. This does not mean rushing into deals without proper analysis, but it does mean moving forward with confidence and purpose. Each action you take brings you closer to your goals.

Building a support network can also enhance your success. Surrounding yourself with knowledgeable professionals, such as lenders, property managers, and advisors, provides valuable insights and support. Additionally, connecting with other investors can offer new perspectives and opportunities for collaboration. This network becomes an important part of your journey, helping you navigate challenges and identify opportunities.

Another key element is continuous learning. The strategies and tools you have learned in this series provide a strong foundation, but the learning process does not end here. The most successful investors are those who continue to educate themselves, staying informed about market trends, new technologies, and evolving strategies. This commitment to learning ensures that you remain adaptable and continue to grow.

Ultimately, this journey is about more than just financial success. It is about creating opportunities, building security, and designing a life that aligns with your goals and values. Airbnb investing, when approached strategically, provides a powerful vehicle for achieving these outcomes. It allows you to take control of your financial future, building a portfolio that generates income, grows in value, and provides long-term stability.

As you close this chapter and begin the next phase of your journey, remember that success is not defined by a single milestone. It is defined by the consistent application of the principles you have learned, the discipline to stay focused, and the resilience to overcome challenges. By committing to this process, you can turn your knowledge into action, your actions into results, and your results into lasting wealth.

The opportunity is in front of you. The system is in your hands. The only question that remains is how far you are willing to go.

How to Get a Personalized Airbnb Mortgage Loan Review

If you found this book helpful, you may want to see how these strategies apply to your own financial situation and investment goals. Every investor's profile is unique. Property type, location, projected Airbnb income, credit score, available capital, and lending guidelines all impact what loan programs you may qualify for and how your deal can be structured.

The examples in this book are designed to teach how Airbnb mortgage loans work—but your real options can only be determined by reviewing your specific numbers and investment scenario.

You can request a no-obligation Airbnb mortgage loan consultation here:

Email: info@FinibiMortgage.com

A licensed mortgage professional will review your scenario and explain what Airbnb financing options may be available to you, including DSCR loans, Non-QM programs, and alternative qualification strategies based on your property and financial profile.

No cost. No pressure. No obligation.

Sincerely,

Joseph G. Correa

Licensed Mortgage Loan Originator

Finibi Mortgage Inc.

About the Author

Joseph G. Correa is a licensed mortgage broker and the founder of Finibi Mortgage, a Florida-based brokerage specializing in real estate investment financing, Airbnb and short-term rental loans, and alternative lending strategies for investors, entrepreneurs, and self-employed borrowers. With more than two decades of experience in mortgage lending, underwriting, and financial structuring, Joseph has helped thousands of clients secure funding using intelligent, flexible loan strategies designed for modern real estate investing.

Unlike traditional loan officers who focus only on closing transactions, Joseph's approach is rooted in long-term wealth building. He believes that mortgage financing—especially for Airbnb and investment properties—should be used as a strategic tool to generate cash flow, scale portfolios, and create financial independence. His philosophy centers on using leverage intelligently, allowing investors to grow without relying solely on personal income or traditional lending limitations.

Joseph is widely recognized for his expertise in DSCR loans, Non-QM lending, short-term rental financing, bank statement programs, and creative deal structuring. He specializes in helping investors qualify based on property income rather than personal income, making it possible for beginners, self-employed individuals, and experienced investors to acquire and scale Airbnb portfolios. His ability to simplify complex lending concepts into clear, actionable strategies has empowered countless individuals to enter the real estate market with confidence.

Joseph created *The Airbnb Mortgage Loan Mastery Series* to give investors the same financing knowledge used by banks, private lenders, and institutional real estate operators. His mission is simple: to help people understand how to qualify, structure deals, and scale using modern lending strategies—so they can build profitable Airbnb businesses and long-term wealth.

When he is not structuring deals or writing, Joseph works directly with investors and borrowers across the United States to design customized financing strategies that align with their goals, property types, and growth plans.

The Airbnb Mortgage Loan Mastery Series Roadmap

The Professional Guide to Financing, Scaling, and Profiting from Short-Term Rental Properties

The purpose of *The Airbnb Mortgage Loan Mastery Series* is to give investors the same financing strategies used by banks, lenders, and institutional real estate operators—translated into clear, practical guidance for everyday investors. Each book builds on the last, taking you from foundational knowledge to advanced deal structuring, portfolio scaling, and long-term wealth creation using Airbnb and short-term rental properties.

Book 1 — Airbnb Mortgage Loan Fundamentals This book gives you the foundation. You will understand how Airbnb mortgage loans work, what makes them different from traditional financing, and how lenders evaluate short-term rental properties. You will learn the core concepts of DSCR, Non-QM loans, and income-based qualification, along with who qualifies and how to structure your first deal. Every book that follows builds on this knowledge and shows you how to apply it to real-world investing.

Book 2 — DSCR Airbnb Mortgage Loans This book focuses on one of the most powerful tools in Airbnb investing: DSCR loans. You will learn how to qualify using rental income instead of personal income, how DSCR is calculated using short-term rental data, and how to position your property to meet lender requirements. This book shows you how to break free from traditional income limitations and scale faster.

Book 3 — Airbnb Mortgage Loans for Beginners This book is designed for first-time investors. You will learn how to buy your first Airbnb property using the right loan strategy, how to analyze deals, and how to overcome common obstacles. It provides a clear, step-by-step path from zero experience to your first successful investment.

Book 4 — Airbnb Investment Property Mortgage Loans This book focuses on scaling. You will learn how to finance multiple Airbnb properties, build a portfolio, and optimize cash flow. It introduces strategies for acquiring properties efficiently and managing them as part of a larger system.

Book 5 — Airbnb Mortgage Loans with No Income Verification

This book explores advanced qualification strategies. You will learn how to get approved without tax returns using DSCR, bank statement, and alternative documentation programs. It is designed for self-employed borrowers and investors who want flexibility in how they qualify.

Book 6 — Luxury Airbnb Mortgage Loans
This book focuses on high-end properties. You will learn how to finance luxury Airbnb investments, analyze high average daily rates, and balance risk with return. It introduces jumbo loan strategies and premium market positioning.

Book 7 — Airbnb Mortgage Loans for Vacation Homes
This book explains how to finance second homes and convert them into profitable short-term rentals. You will learn the difference between second home and investment property guidelines, along with hybrid usage strategies and compliance considerations.

Book 8 — Airbnb Mortgage Loan Refinancing & Cash-Out Strategies
This book teaches you how to unlock equity and scale faster. You will learn how to refinance Airbnb properties, execute cash-out strategies, and recycle capital into new investments.

Book 9 — Airbnb Mortgage Loans for Multi-Unit Properties
This book focuses on duplexes, triplexes, and small multifamily properties. You will learn how to finance multiple income streams within one property, analyze mixed rental models, and navigate zoning and compliance.

Book 10 — Advanced Airbnb Mortgage Loan Structuring

This book brings everything together. You will learn how to combine DSCR, asset-based, and creative financing strategies to close complex deals. It is designed for investors who want to operate at a high level and scale without limits.

This series is designed to be followed step by step or used as a reference based on your current stage. Whether you are just starting or already building a portfolio, each book provides the tools, strategies, and insights needed to move forward with clarity and confidence.

The goal is simple: to help you understand how to finance, structure, and scale Airbnb investments so you can build a profitable, long-term real estate business.

Educational & Financial Disclaimer

This book is provided for educational and informational purposes only. The author and publisher are not engaged in rendering legal, tax, accounting, investment, or financial advice. Although Joseph G. Correa is a licensed mortgage loan originator, the information in this book is intended to provide general education about Airbnb mortgage loans, DSCR financing, and short-term rental investment strategies—not personalized financial, legal, or lending advice.

Mortgage programs, underwriting guidelines, interest rates, credit requirements, and short-term rental financing options vary by lender, investor, state, and economic conditions, and may change at any time without notice. The examples, calculations, and scenarios presented in this book are hypothetical and are for illustration purposes only. They do not represent guaranteed results, loan approvals, or actual investment outcomes.

Short-term rental performance, including Airbnb income, occupancy rates, and average daily rates, is influenced by market demand, competition, seasonality, management quality, and local regulations. These factors can vary significantly and are not guaranteed. Before making any financial decisions—including purchasing an Airbnb property, applying for a DSCR or Non-QM loan, refinancing, or using real estate financing for investment purposes—readers should consult with a qualified mortgage professional, financial advisor, tax advisor, or attorney who can evaluate their specific situation.

Risk Disclosure

Real estate investing and short-term rental financing involve risk. Airbnb properties rely on variable income, which can fluctuate due to changes in demand, competition, economic conditions, and local regulations. There is no guarantee that a property will achieve projected income levels or maintain consistent occupancy.

Borrowing to purchase or refinance investment properties increases financial leverage and risk. Failure to make required mortgage payments could result in foreclosure or loss of property. DSCR and Non-QM loans may carry higher interest rates, stricter terms, or prepayment penalties, which can impact long-term profitability.

Additionally, changes in laws or regulations governing short-term rentals may affect your ability to operate a property as an Airbnb. Investors are responsible for ensuring compliance with all local, state, and federal regulations.

This book teaches structured, strategic, and responsible approaches to Airbnb financing and investing, but no strategy is risk-free. Readers are solely responsible for their financial decisions and outcomes. Neither the author nor the publisher makes any warranties, express or implied, regarding the accuracy, completeness, or applicability of the information in this book to any individual situation.

www.ingramcontent.com/pod-product-compliance
Lightning Source LLC
LaVergne TN
LVHW022221200926
848481LV00006B/2064